Letters to a daughter

Hubert Bland

Letters to a daughter

Copyright © 2023 Bibliotech Press
All rights reserved

The present edition is a reproduction of previous publication of this classic work. Minor typographical errors may have been corrected without note; however, for an authentic reading experience the spelling, punctuation, and capitalization have been retained from the original text.

ISBN: 979-8-88830-382-5

TO

ROSAMUND

"More dear to me than are the ruddy drops
That visit my sad heart."

CONTENTS

ON LIFE AT LARGE

Oct. 17, 19—.

My dear Alexa,—

You asked me to write to you while you were away—"long letters," you said; and the request set me wondering a little. I think I understand now. Comprehension came to me in a flash as I was stropping my razor this morning: the sharpening of one thing helped to sharpen another—my wits. You felt, didn't you, that as I am a writing sort of man, I might, in long letters, find it possible to say things that an impalpable something had hitherto made it difficult for me to say when you and I were face to face? I think, perhaps, you were right; these long letters will show. All the same, we have been as intimate as most fathers and daughters; more intimate, I fondly think.

I should like to write at length to-day; about 2000 words—forgive the jargon of the trade—on the relations of father and grown-up daughter, but you asked for letters, not essays. Still, I might point out this, in case it has not occurred to you before:—Those relations are peculiar, more than that, unique. His daughter is the only woman in all the world for whom a man five-and-twenty years her senior can feel no stir of passion, no trace of that complex emotion that modern novelists and people of that sort are so pleased to call sex-love; the only woman from whom he cannot possibly evoke passion in return. That fact of itself gives his daughter a chamber all to herself in the man's heart, a chamber guarded by an angel with a flaming sword.

1

To talk of love is the next thing to making love, they say, or something like that. It is probably not quite true; but now that I come to think of it, when I have talked of love to women whom I knew well, after a quarter of an hour or so a certain tartness, a certain uncomfortableness has come into the talk, also one felt oneself becoming just a trifle artificial, less entirely frank, less spontaneous, than one likes to be. Such talks have ended not infrequently in tears and temper. I need not assure you, Alexa, that the tears were not mine: as for the temper! And when I have talked of love to women whom I have not known well I have sensed a sort of agitation on both sides which seemed to portend danger in the not dim distance. One never felt quite sure as to what might happen in the next five minutes. Of course, all this refers to a long time ago. You will understand that. There is some truth in the old saying evidently. You might remember it. But the point of these remarks, as Mr. Bunsby says (it is one of your merits that you are not ashamed to love Dickens), lies in the application of them. His daughter is the one young woman to whom a man can talk of love quit of the faintest fear of being led into making it. I probably shall talk of love in these long letters you asked me to write. I am not sure but what, in any other mood and on any other day but this, I should have said that between men and women there is nothing else worth talking about. But if I said that now, I should be insincere, for I don't feel it. This autumn weather, this dismal lingering death of summer, oppress my soul, and one should be in high fettle to talk intelligently of love. Now I am not that to-day as I look out of the library window and see those big funereal cedars lords of all, the whole garden subdued to their sombre humour. Day and night the piteous leaves of all the other trees are falling, falling like slow rain-drops; and at twilight they sound upon the garden paths as the footsteps of ghosts might sound—creepy, creepy. This morning I picked a rose for sheer pity of it, and in half an hour its charm was gone; its very colour had changed, its pink shell-like petals (it was the last of the Maman Cochets) had turned livid as the lips of a corpse; it exhaled, not perfume, but an odour of death. The birds flutter about aimlessly, they seem to feel there is nothing left for them to do in a world so full of sadness, no nests to be builded, no broods to be reared; and they haven't the heart to sing. To add the last touch of sable to the whole mumpish outlook, you are away. Don't think that insincere: it is not a bit. I wandered moodily, and with no definite object, into your room to-day. It was in shocking disorder, untidiness appalling, of course, or it had not been yours; but somehow the chaos did not irritate me as it usually does. Somehow I was glad of it. Had it been otherwise—as neat as my own study, for instance—I had been plunged into still deeper gloom. It was like an empty nursery in which the toys were still lying scattered all about. Oh, the deathly chill of an empty and tidy nursery!

Let me see, you are nineteen or a trifle more, aren't you? And Love must be lying in wait for you somewhere very near by. I wonder whether you will know him when you see him. If you do, then will you be the cleverest of your sex, and much cleverer than any one of mine. If he is anything at all like the Love of the Christmas cards and the funny little poets who like to display a smattering of classic knowledge—have no fear of him whatever. He won't hurt, that chubby child with the toy bow and arrows. Of what drivelling folly, what stupendous ignorance were they guilty who personified Love as a pink and pulpy baby nourished on Pott's Emulsion! Don't believe them, dear. When Love's self comes he comes always a strong man armed—a warrior with old scars upon his forehead and dints upon his shield. And there is another mailed adventurer, too, who may likely spring upon you unawares. He is so like Love in his equipment and in the manner of his attack, this one, that it is not until forty years have passed that one can see through his disguise. He is, by the most, held to be unmentionable between men of my age and women of yours, but the name of him is Passion. If I were an ideal instead of a practicable, work-a-day parent, I should warn you against him in the solemnest way, or I should pretend that there was no such a person. But I don't do either; first because I know the warning and the conventional lie would be futile, and next, because I don't think either would be quite fair to you. This world is an interesting place; it would be considerably less interesting but for Passion's vagaries, his adroit ambushes, his sudden swift assaults, his slow retirements, and, sometimes, his unexpected defeats. And I want you to find life interesting—you are sure not to find it happy, folk of our temperament never do. Here I should like to drop metaphor and dissertate for a while in the plain language of what some modern writers call "psycho-physiology," but I don't want to startle you, much less to shock, so I will reserve psycho-physiology for another time. This, however, I may say: you will know Love from Passion just by this—that Love wants ever to give; Passion, to take. When the two appear as close allies—well, then you will be upon the eve of certainly the most momentous and, perhaps, the most catastrophic event of all your life. There is really no saying what may happen then, and you had better come and talk it over quietly with me. Don't be afraid of Passion because you have heard him called by uglier names, and remember always this—

that come he by tempestuous assault or by patient siege he never wins of his own strength alone. It is always a traitor within the gates that gives the citadel away. That's the one you have to keep an eye on—the traitor inside.

I have often heard you say (you are the only woman I have heard say it) that you would not, if you could, be a man. I like you the better for saying it, but you are wrong all the same; at least I think so. Whether men or women have the better time I don't know, but I do know that men have the safer. They get more out of life, and they risk infinitely less in the getting thereof. In this matter of Passion, for instance (the metaphor's changed now), the handicap is quite infernally unfair. It almost makes a just man blaspheme the handicapper. It is as though the two sexes were skating. Each equally enjoys the exhilarating exercise. To mine a slip means, at the worst, a ridiculous posture for a moment or two and a few bruises; to yours, the almost certainty of a compound fracture, possibly of a broken back. But perhaps in a sporting spirit you will reply, the deadlier peril carries with it the keener thrill; and really there may be something in that. My observation of life, however, convinces me to the contrary. For me the chances of the undignified tumble and the bruises are enough. Some of your advanced sisters (you'll meet them presently, if not in the flesh, then in books) will tell you that the tendencies of the times are all in favour of equalising the chances. Maybe; but put not your trust in tendencies, Alexa. Think what you like, but act as though the world were going to be always just what it is now. Pioneers are always uncomfortable, and for that reason, mostly unpleasant. Your business is to make life interesting, and in so far as you do that you yourself will be an interesting woman. At the same time, an you love me, don't imagine that I am counselling cowardice or even prudence. If cowardice be a positive vice, prudence is but a negative virtue, and the line that divides the two is so thin as to be often imperceptible. As you travel through life you will find the negative virtues, the cloistered virtues, as Milton, I think it is, calls them, about the least amiable and the most irritating things you will encounter. No, don't be a coward. No woman with a chin like yours, and the brain I feel sure you have inherited, need be that. No end of obstacles and hindrances will go down before that chin of yours if only you thrust it forward at the exactly right moment; realities as well as unrealities, your living fellow creatures and the ghosts of dead ideas. Before such a chin many a seeming lion in the path will turn into naught more fearsome than a spitting kitten after all; still kittens, it is worth remembering, can scratch. And scratches disfigure.

Try to avoid scratches: they smart, and there is no honour in the scars thereof. Make the world interesting to yourself, as I charged you before, and make it comfortable. To do that is about the most one can hope to do 'twixt swaddling clothes and shroud. I don't ask you to venerate other people's prejudices—scorn them as much as you like; but I do advise you to respect their power. Bow reverentially in the House of Rimmon. Try to imagine yourself (the effort will not be very great after you have looked around you for a while) a civilised being cast among savages. The savages have, of course, some rigid rules of conduct, of the origin of which they know nothing and which, for that very reason, they hold in the deeper awe. The breaking of a rule involves a slow scraping to death with oyster shells, and yet such breaking gives a good deal of comfort and satisfaction to you; there is a thrill about it somewhere. "Que faire" then? Stick to the rules like the most besotted savage of them all? Not a bit of it; break them just when and how it suits you and then use your superior intelligence. You will get a poignant and penetrating pleasure from the mere exercise of your higher faculty. I am not sure but that that alone will not be reward sufficient. All this sounds like a lengthy way of restating the old eleventh commandment, I know; but, indeed, it is something more than that, it is rather an intelligent criticism of some of the ten and a reasonable justification of that odd one.

My advice assumes, of course, that you are a Superior Person. I think I have noted certain traits in you which convince me that that is rather your view of yourself. Well, even so, you probably know little of yourself, but yet more than any one else knows of you. You see you are the one most nearly interested in the diagnosis. Time will test the correctness of your judgment; but when he has had long enough to form an opinion it will not matter much to you what his opinion is. But of Time's dealings with your sex I shall have something to say anon. Some one has said that the bitterest of all regrets is that for the sins we have not committed. That is mere cynical ineptitude.

It is not the memory of omitted sins, but the recollection of lost chances that writhes and rankles.

Always, my dear Alexa,
Your didactic but most affectionate friend and
Father

ON GOING TO CHURCH

Oct. 28, 19—

My dear Alexa,—

Some commonplace person has said that the really important part of a woman's letter is always in the postscript. It pains me to recognise how often the commonplace is also the true. It is the postscript of your pleasant letter that I must answer to-day. "Ought I to go to church?" you ask, and I can't think why you say "ought." "Ought" is a word which you know irritates me. It suggests Ethical Societies and their preposterous hymns. It raises questions of "right and wrong," and I feel that at my age one should be done with questions of that disturbing kind. And the worst of it is I don't quite know what you mean, for you may mean one of two things. It may be a very little question or a very big one you are putting. Well, I will try to deal with both. If you mean ought you to go to church on Sunday just now, when you are staying with correct people who go themselves, then I answer most emphatically "Yes." To begin with it is a mere act of politeness. You might as well ask "Ought I to dress for dinner?" But it is something more than that. To stay away from church when your host and his friends go is to challenge after-luncheon controversy, to invite a religious polemic. It is to advertise in the most vulgar and objectionable way possible your irreligion, or, if not that exactly, at least your religious doubts. It is to make yourself prominent and prickly.

But I can't believe you mean that. A child of mine may have prickles, but I am happily confident that she would carefully

8

conceal them. What I think you do mean is, "Is it wise, in order to make the best of life, to cultivate the religious emotions?" That was it, wasn't it? "Ought I to go to church?" was only your succinct and symbolical way of putting it. It was neatly put, and I congratulate you, Alexa.

Well, it is a big question, as I said, but one that is comparatively easy to answer, for the answer is obvious. It may take a long time answering but that is the worst of the obvious: it always does take such a long time stating, whereas the non-obvious may generally be put into an epigram. Who are the nicest people you know, Alexa; the people you like best to talk to; the people whose judgment you most rely on; the gayest people; the people who have the art of treating serious things lightly and light things with a becoming seriousness; the all round people; the people whose opinion you would most value of a poem, a novel, a symphony, a landscape; the people whose taste you trust? Think now, are they not in almost every case people with some sort of religious belief? Or, to put it otherwise, have you ever met a really delightful Atheist, man or woman? You have met many worthy Atheists, I know, persons whose moral code was as conspicuous as a red nose, whose admirable qualities stuck out of them like hat-pins, persons you are almost bound in common decency to respect; but have they been delightful? Were you not always conscious of a want in them somewhere, just as you are conscious of something lacking in a person who has no ear for music, or who does not like olives?

The religious instinct, the craving to get into touch with something outside the material world, beyond the things we see or apprehend with any of our five senses is born in us just like

9

any other instinct. The history of mankind is proof positive of the fact. We have never yet caught a primitive man—most savages are degenerates they say; but, depend upon it, if ever we do we shall find him going "to church," as you would put it. Even if we didn't, even if it could be demonstrated beyond possibility of doubt that our arboreal ancestor knew naught of religious emotion, but was contented with his wives and his cocoanuts, it would be no disproof of my assertion that we, the people of 19—, are born with the religious instinct. There are exceptions of course, freaks, just as there are unfortunates born without drums to their ears and without a liking for the scent of tonkin beans; but we need not bother about them. You, my child, have drums to your ears, you keep a tonkin bean in your glove-box, and you have the religious instinct. The question I am answering, remember, is: ought you, Alexa, to go to church? In other words, then, it amounts to this: ought you to suppress an instinct? It is a question surely which answers itself. The pleasures of life consist in the gratification of instincts, either inherited or cultivated. To suppress an instinct, then, or to allow it to atrophy by disuse, is to shut oneself off from an opportunity of pleasure, to narrow the range of one's emotions and one's intellect, to diminish the number of one's sensations; it is to be incomplete, and if you are incomplete, you cannot be delightful, Alexa. Your favourite Heine says somewhere that a charming woman without religion is like a beautiful flower without perfume. He was always right when he wrote of women. So am I.

But I think I hear you asking, is it true that the religious emotions are necessarily always pleasurable? Was it pleasure that St Simeon Stylites felt upon his pillar? Does the missionary experience a delightful thrill while the savage is skinning him alive? Well, I am not sure. I am inclined to think that St Simeon did enjoy that cold eminence of his, at any rate more than he was capable of enjoying anything else. As for the missionary, I did meet one once who had been partially skinned, and strangely enough, he was just on the eve of starting to pay another visit to the interesting island folk who had flayed him; so we must presume it was not so bad after all. But even were it otherwise, my reply would be that persons like St Simeon have cultivated their religious emotions overmuch, and have paid insufficient attention to the other sides of their nature. They are like gluttons, or drunkards, or profligates, or the musically mad. They are religious debauchees. To spend all one's time in religious exercises is as bad, and as foolish in its way, as to be perpetually playing the piano: it is wasting your own life and making yourself a nuisance to your neighbours. Prayer is good, my child, but really I think I would as soon see you always on your head as always on your knees. There is a line of a hymn which speaks of Heaven as a place

> *"Where congregations ne'er break up*
> *And Sabbaths have no end."*

but that was written, we may be sure, by a religious debauchee. He was a glutton, that fellow. Now, in this, as in all other things, I would have my daughter be an epicure—not a greedy pig. Talking of Epicurus, by the way, I feel sure that if Epicurus were alive in London to-day he would attend the services in the Chapter House of the New Cathedral almost daily. Yes, and not as a mere listener to music: he would absorb the atmosphere of the place; he would be of the most devout. After all, the proof of the pudding is in the eating, isn't it?—and in the eupeptic tranquillity that follows. You can put the thing to a practical and a personal test if you will. Go, sit as much by yourself as you can in some great church—a cathedral for choice, of course; choose some corner where the light is broken by a stained-glass window—the glass must not be of date later than the end of the sixteenth century—and stay there quietly until after the service ends. Let the music of the organ, the clear voices of the choir boys, the penetrating odour of the incense, work their will upon you. Surrender yourself wholly, uncritically, to the influence of the place, and then, when it is all over, and you are the last to leave, or the last but one, say—for it were well, it were perfect if, as you cross the chancel, you should see one wimpled nun "breathless in adoration" before the altar—write and ask me again, if you can, ought you to go to church!

Ah, but you, or some other girl who, unlike you, is a little agnostic Philistine, might say, those emotional experiences are æsthetic, not religious. It is the music itself that thrills, not the devotion that the music seeks to express; it is the particles of the incense that titillate the nostrils, not the odour of prayer that penetrates to the soul. Not a bit of it, Alexa, that is a callow observation worthy only a Hall of Science lecturer. Listen to exactly the same music played by the same hands, sung by the same voices, in the Queen's Hall, and see if the emotional effect upon yourself is in any sense the same. It will charm you, of course, but there will be something missing—and that something is the satisfaction of the religious instinct, the response of the Unseen to our craving for relations with it. Yes, but the church itself, the building, the pointed arches, the clustered columns, the groined roof—have not all these much to do with the psychological effect? Of course they have. But then the church was builded of men who had cultivated their religious instincts: men who believed, who felt: the building fits the religious idea as perfectly as I hope your latest frock fits your frame, my kiddie. What is a great cathedral but the religious emotion expressed in stone?

"And yet—it mayn't be true," I hear you mutter, with a little sceptical tremor of the lips. I don't quite know what you mean by "it," and I don't greatly care. To define "it," would require a big book, wouldn't it? It has already required big libraries full of big books—and still the foolish squabble. There It is all the time. So we will let that question pass. What is true, what is a fact as palpable as, more palpable than, the improvement in the Strand, is the existence in us, in you, of the religious instinct—of a craving for personal relations with the Unseen, as I said. Not to seek to gratify that were as foolish as to refuse to listen to a Beethoven sonata because you feel doubtful whether Beethoven ever lived—whether all his music were not written by another gentleman of the same name.

Your mother asks me to tell you that she thinks you ought sometimes to write to her. "Ought," and again "ought" and always "ought" in this beast of a world!

Your devoted and truly religious
Father

ON BEING DELIGHTFUL

Nov. 8, 19—.

My dear Alexa,—

You accuse me of perpetually charging you to be delightful, and of never giving you any detailed and specific instructions as to how to be it. I can't help feeling that the accusation is more than a little unjust, that is to say, I did suffer under a sense of injustice for a quarter of an hour or so. It seemed to me that although I had never taught you by way of precept, by way of example I had not failed, for I have been extremely charming to you, Alexa. But reflection has caused me to realise that, perhaps, nay certainly, you are right. Many of the qualities that make a man charming are the antipodes of those which render a woman delightful. There are a few, of course, that should be common to both, but they are few. I will not trifle with the subject and do outrage to your common sense by telling you that Nature herself will teach you to be delightful, because I remember that you and I long ago, when you were little more than a kiddie, agreed that delightfulness is the one attribute which Nature never possesses, and, therefore, can never transmit to her children. Nature is all sorts of pleasant things. She is wholesome, for instance, impressive, restorative, not infrequently magnificent—just here and now she is damp and abominably depressing—but she is never delightful. Delightfulness is an achievement of art. One may speak, accurately, of a delightful garden; none but an indiscriminating idiot would talk of a delightful wilderness. An alcove decorated with tact and lighted, or half-lighted—better—

with Chinese lanterns, might be delightful: a sunset never could be. Therefore, my daughter, if you follow the promptings of Nature you may be, let us say, astonishing, but you will never be delightful or anything like it.

Personally, I think you are delightful already; but then, I am quite conscious that that view of mine may be a paternal parti pris which other people with blunter perceptions than mine may possibly not share. If you wish to be universally delightful then, you must be prepared to make of yourself a work of Art. Nature, happily for you—I may say this without flattery—has given you the materials; it is for you to work them up, remembering that a naturally-gifted young woman is no more a delightful young woman than a box of colours is a picture.

In the eighties, when the Æsthetic Movement, as it was absurdly called, was on the town, we used to talk a good deal, of "Art for Art's sake." It was a phrase that gave grave offence to the Philistine, (that was why we used it so constantly), the Philistine who nosed in it a danger to his own peculiar variety of morals. You don't often hear it now, for the Philistine was too strong for us, and he has conquered. And yet it was a phrase as innocent as it was apt. It summed up in four words—nay, in three, for one is repeated—a true and imperishable principle. All it meant was that Art should seek no end outside itself: that if you set about painting a picture, say, your aim should be just to paint a beautiful picture, not to inculcate moral habits in a Sunday school, or to boil your own pot by achieving the line in Burlington House, or even the gold medal of the Salon. You see the implication, Alexa? You see how "Art for Art's sake" applies to you just now? If you are going to practise the art of being delightful you must do it for the sake of being delightful, not with any arrière pensée, not with an eye to the best partners at dances or invitations to the mansions of the affluent. To die with the consciousness of all your life long having been a delightful person! Can anything be better than that, save living with the same consciousness? Moreover, I can't help thinking that the best of all preparations for the next world is to be as nice as one possibly can in this.

You know a good deal; a good deal of many things, I have seen to that. But it would be well rather to conceal than to display your knowledge. There is nothing people in general like so little in woman as knowledge, and when I say people in general I mean people of both sexes. So you must never put all the goods in the shop window, or, at any rate, not all at once. Show just as many as, and those of the sort that, will attract the particular gazer in the window at the time. Therefore, affect an ignorance if you have it not, remembering that the more you really do know the easier is it to appear not to know it. This seems an unreasonable injunction, and therefore I will give you my reason for proffering it. Broadly speaking, human nature suffers from a passion to be instructive. We all love to teach, to tell things. Particularly do men love to tell things to young women. I have often had a man come up to me and say "Miss So-and-So is a charming girl," just after I have been noticing that the charm for him consisted wholly in the interested and receptive manner with which she had been listening, or affecting to listen, to such information as he had delighted to impart. Whenever a man talks to a young woman he tries his best to appear a little bigger all round than he knows himself to be. Unexpectedly to check his enterprise by showing that you know as much as he does has pretty much the same effect upon his mind as though you were suddenly to add twenty years to your age, to discover wrinkles, or to develop a squint. Of course, I do not mean that when a man is "telling you things" you should sit mumchance and, as it were, dumfounded at his erudition. A few well-directed and intelligent questions will help you vastly. But take care that the questions are such as you feel pretty confident he will be able to answer. Here I can speak to you from the depths of my own experience. When a pretty young woman asks me something that I don't know, I feel more inclined to box her ears than to kiss her.

Learn early, dear student of life, to suffer bores gladly. Remember that in so doing you are making yourself delightful, not only to the poor bore, but also doubly delightful to the other persons present from whom you have drawn him off.

Get as quickly as possible out of the way of speaking of yourself, even of regarding yourself as "a girl." You are, I know, only nineteen now, or is it twenty?—and there is not much harm in it so far—but one day you will be five-and-twenty, and then it will sound, and will be, ridiculous. Girlishness of speech, of thought and of manner is a habit easily acquired and with difficulty dropped. Let others think of you and speak of you as a girl if they will, but don't do it yourself as you hope for delightfulness. There are few things in a small way that give the wise and fastidious man a nastier jar than to hear a woman well away towards the end of her third decade refer to herself as a "girl." It is the fashion of folks nowadays to try to defer their children's womanhood as long as possible—one constantly hears it remarked, "how much younger women are than they used to be!" Don't believe it, Alexa, they are just the same age as ever they were. We cannot, do what we will, keep our daughters young. We can keep them silly, but we can't keep them young. Great is Art, but Nature beats her there. Besides, this in your ear! Just as it is hateful to hear a mature young woman call herself a girl, so it is delightful to hear one who really is a girl speak of herself as a woman. I cannot tell you why—I think I know, but it would take too long just now, and the psychology of it is subtle extremely—but trust me in this, it is so.

Never if you can help it let a man do for you anything you have reason to believe he will not like doing—anything which you think you would not like to do were you he and were he you. As a practical instance: If you happen to be bicycle-riding with a man, don't let him drag you up the hills, or against the wind. Even at some inconvenience to yourself refuse the proffered aid of his shoulder, of a bit of rope, or the waistband of his Norfolk jacket. The aid will be proffered as a matter of conventional courtesy, but the fellow's heart will not be in it. He will like you ever so much the better if you assert your independence; unless, of course, he be intensely young, and then he doesn't count. When I was a young man I once went skating with a very charming young woman who told me she could skate, and that she enjoyed the fun of it. I found she couldn't skate—she could only sprawl about and tumble down when unsupported. I had to spend the whole of that glorious afternoon—I can smell the perfume of the pines which stood around the lake even now across nearly half a century of time—in upholding her until my arms and ankles ached. It was the only day of hard ice that winter. That girl was not your mother, my child. After that day she never could by any possibility have become your mother.

When I set out on that skating expedition I was half in love with her; when I came home I wasn't! Selfish? Yes—well!

Now for a really unworldly piece of counsel. Don't be at too much trouble to acquire or to cultivate the acquaintance or the friendship of the rich. In the mix-up that goes on to-day you will meet them, of course—but they are seldom worth the bother. There is little or nothing worth having to be got from them. And the fact that you have made yourself even a trifle more agreeable to a rich man or woman than you would have done to a poor person, is sure, sooner or later, to inflict upon you a feeling of self-despite, of self-humiliation. It is as well to have as few of those sorts of feelings as possible. A visit to a house much bigger than one's own, overflowing with butlers, so to speak, is but poor recompense for the very smallest scratch to one's self-respect. A woman with scars on her self-respect is never quite delightful. You will find it easier to be delightful to men than to women. With men, over and above the cultivated charm of your art, you have always your sex—that potent mystery—to trust to. With women it tells rather against than for you. Therefore double your efforts to be delightful to women. In this matter I can give you none of the specific details you ask for. To them apply the golden rule—do unto women as you would have women do unto you. You will meet many fool-women—whom in your heart and brain you will contemn—but remember that the veriest fool-woman of them all will probably be clever enough to know exactly when and where to stick her claws into the other woman. Avoid those claws, my child.

Your devoted
Father

THE GLAMOUR OF THE FOOTLIGHTS

Dec. 5, 19—.

My dear Alexa,—

I was delighted to get your long letter on Monday. It was just the sort of letter I like to have, from a woman especially: a letter with naught impersonal in it, full of the familiar and intimate turns of phrase. I fancied I could hear the very inflection of your voice here and there. That is the way to write; to write to a friend, I mean. Try hard to remember all the time that you are not writing to a newspaper, or labouring to produce what, at school, used to be called "a meritorious composition." Avoid the cliché as you would the devil; nay, even more; for he, in some of his moods, might be interesting; the cliché is always tiresome. Your letter caught me in a moment of depression, one of those mopish moments which come upon me oftener than they should of late, and lie like shadows upon the spirit's surface, turning to monotone what should be all iridescence. I went down into the breakfast-room and fired off an epigram. It is true I had already perfected and polished that epigram while I lay wakeful in the dead waste and middle of the night, but I should never have summoned energy enough to part with it so soon had it not been for your letter. It was not appreciated. The bacon had been served on a coldish dish. So you see you are responsible for that wilful waste of a good thing, Alexa; a thing that would have (and mayhap will yet) set the club smoking-room in a titter. At the breakfast-table it raised only an acidulous smile, the merest flicker. The family looked reprovingly at me for beginning the day so frivolously. Had you been there, now! That is one of your chiefest charms, my daughter, that is why I love you so; you always appreciate your father's efforts to pervert the truth.

There was one thing in your letter that troubled me a little though, because I fancied I saw in it a symptom, a foreshadowing, so to speak, like the sore throat and little dry cough that herald an attack of scarlet fever. Do you remember when you had scarlet fever and what a pale ghost your father was for seven dreadful days until the danger was over and gone? Ah me! But as to this symptom. It was only two lines in which you said something—I don't remember exactly what, and I have not your letter by me at the moment—about your "favourite actor." You did not mention the fellow's name, and I thank you for that. It has probably saved me from the crime of assassination. Think how disgusting it would have been! I don't mean the assassination itself, that would have been jolly, but the newspaper boys bawling up and down the Strand, "Horrible murder of Cyril, or Claude, or Basil Somebody-or-other!" And your poor mother in tears at home; and then the squalid Old Bailey, and the glib counsel, and the solemn ass on the Bench, and the unsympathetic stodgers in the jury box. I feel I could never survive a criminal trial. My spirit would break through its fleshly casings, and flee away from the deadly commonplaceness of the thing before it was half over. Therefore in the days of your youth look not upon the mimes to admire them, Alexa, and bring not your father's gray hairs in sorrow to the dock.

But to return to seriousness and that symptom I spoke of. I have noticed lately in several young women of your age, though I am glad to say not in you, an unsalutary tendency to exalt the mummer. I have heard them chatter to each other about him in the drawing-room, here; I am told (Jane tells me in fact, she tells me unblushingly) that they buy his photographs, sometimes as many as three or four of one of him in different costumes; that they stick these photographs up on their bedroom mantelpieces, and that in some desperate cases, they write him letters asking for his autograph, and even go the length of sending him flowers. Flowers! They had far better send onions.

I will not let myself think hardly of these maidens of our day. I feel I must recognise that after all they are but doing what the young males of their species always have done and still do. The glamour of the footlights has always tempted youth to make a donkey of itself. Young men of a like age talk actress over their cheap cigars, spend their sparse shillings on photographs of legs, and go the full length of their limited credit in flower shops. But, then, they are young men, you see, and that makes all the difference. It does, I assure you, and my fondest hope is that the discovery that it does may not come upon you as a shock. There may be no reason, "in justice," why there should be one law for women and another for men, but just now there is, and if ever there isn't what a deuce of a world it will be! Let me imagine an instance of what I mean. If a few years hence I were to come upon your brother John with his arm round a dairymaid (I shall not, for dairymaids are buried in the picturesque past) I should give him a talking to, but the amorous incident would not break my night's rest. But if, oh my child—if I caught you kissing the postman! There, you see. I know quite well you are ill-treating that pretty mobile under-lip of yours at the indelicate suggestion. "Indelicate," I feel sure that is the word you will use.

And it is, that is just what I mean it to be. Well, there is something indelicate in this fuss about the actor fellow.

I don't like doing it, but for once let me pose before you as laudator temporis acti. You were pretty good at Latin a year ago, and you still keep enough of it to translate that. I can't conceal from myself that there has been a change, and a change not for the better, in the emotional atmosphere of the young woman; it has become soppy, stuffy; if I were to say sniffy I should not say too much, but I won't say quite that. Young women have always fallen in love—I use the phrase in its widest, vaguest sense—with Man, with just the male creature. Had they not we should none of us be here, I suppose. When that nebulous emotion becomes more definite, concentrates itself and gets directed at a particular member of the species, it becomes Love, the real thing, the motive power of life, the subject matter of poetry, of drama, of legend, of art generally. But in its vague state it hovers over Man, just Man. Obviously it must be over Man in some more or less definite form. Well, now, what I wanted to say was this. Once upon a time, not so long ago either, young women "fell in love" with, made a fuss over, Man in his more heroic, more intensely masculine and vigorous aspects. It was the soldier, the sailor, the adventurer of all sorts, that appealed to their tenderest susceptibilities. Even the highwayman was held a romantic figure. Many a nice girl has tossed a bouquet or waved a damp pocket-handkerchief at a highwayman on his last drive to Tyburn Tree. Women upon whom one must not be too hard have before now eloped with their grooms. I say "upon whom one must not be too hard," because after all grooming is a man's trade. Personable prize-fighters, too, have had their share of delicate feminine attentions. Now all these types of manhood,—

and, remember, it is the type more than the individual who first appeals to those vague unsettled amatory emotions we are talking about,—were male things who did something, something mostly that had danger in it, that called for a spice of hardihood, of courage, of some honest, manly, simple quality in the doing. Venus, you know, 'tis said, gave herself to Mars, and tried it on—the hussy—with a robust young hunter; but scandal does not connect even her name with a mummer's!

Now, this change in the young woman's emotional outlook from the hero, of sorts, to the actor, is a change I can't help feeling to be for the worse. For, you see, the object of the emotional outpouring is no longer a man who does something, but only a man who pretends to do something, who postures and poses and plays at doing something! "The Captain with his whiskers" of whom our grandmothers sang, and at whom our mothers were not allowed to peep through the slats of their Venetian blinds, may have been a bit of a dog, not "a marrying man," mayhap, as another old song had it; but at least his scarlet jacket and his gold lace stood for something, for something worth having. That scarlet was smoke-blackened at Waterloo, that gold lace lost its lustre on the slopes at Inkerman. Girls don't sing "The Captain with his whiskers" now, and, to tell you the truth, I'm rather glad of that. May I not live to see the day, though I am afraid I shall, when they will hymn the seductions of "The actor with his grease pot."

Please understand—but I need not ask that, you always do understand me, you are the only woman who ever has, and consequently made the right allowances—that I do not say one word in contempt of the actor's profession as such. It is an arduous trade, and as honest as any other whose object is to amuse the public. They call it an "art" now, I notice, and, perhaps it is, a kind of a sort of an art; but my point is that it is not a business that calls out the best, the virile, from a man. On the other hand, it does evoke, by the confession of lots of actors and actresses themselves, the malign qualities of personal vanity, petty jealousy, and peacockiness. The constant assumption of other personalities does and must wipe out such personality as the man may have to begin with. If you are always pretending to be somebody else you must inevitably lose your own self at last. And then, it is so quite awfully an affair of clothes; of clothes and of powdered wigs, and of shaven faces and smirks. Now, I put it to you, Alexa, do you think a delightful woman ought to fall in love with a suit of clothes bought in Covent Garden? Further, do you think she can be really delightful if she does?

After all, perhaps, the change is not so great, or the thing so serious as it seems. Perhaps, when all's said and done, it is only the actor in his character of hero with whom the young woman "falls in love." There would be a sharp reaction, I make no doubt, did she see the fellow himself in tweeds guzzling brandy and soda in a Strand bar, or even in evening dress sipping champagne at the Savoy. And, to do him justice, sometimes, on the stage, in the glare of the footlights, an actor does look uncommonly like a gentleman. You might almost fancy he was the Sir Rupert Glenalmond or the Lord Archibald Heavyswell he pretends to be. But still it is, while you are about it, better to "fall in love" with the reality than with the sham, isn't it? You must fall in love with something, I know; but let it be with the Man, not with the Mimic.

Therefore, Alexa dear, next time you go to the theatre spend the dressing hour in the cultivation of the critical spirit. That shall save you. Be a modern girl by all means; be as modern as ever you can, and count on my support to the utmost extreme of your modernity, but don't, don't be a little duffer.

Always your affectionate, if, this time, also
Your admonitory
Father

THE RUDENESS OF WOMEN

Dec. 17, 19—.

My dear Alexa,—

As in your last letter you pose me with no puzzling questions on the subject of conduct, I may take it, I suppose, that for the moment, at least, life has become less problematical to you. That is well. Even the youngest and most intelligent of us should cease from bothering now and then, and be content just to be onlookers, to banish that fearsome word "ought" from our vocabularies and from our minds. Conduct, as Matthew Arnold pointed out a long time ago, is three-fourths of life, a biggish fraction, but, after all, a fraction only; and there come periods when we thank our stars for the comparative restfulness of that odd quarter. I often think that Matthew might, with advantage, slightly have expanded his formula. Had he said that conduct is three-fourths of life for three-fourths of life he had been nearer the mark. Men and women, but more often men than women, I fancy, who have passed the third quarter rarely worry themselves as to what they ought, or ought not, to do. They just go ahead and do it, confident that whether the action turn out for weal or for woe it has been decided for them in that other three-quarters left behind and beyond recall or undoing. We spend the greater part of our life in acquiring habits, and the lesser in acquiescent obedience to them. Therefore, if you are to be a delightful middle-aged lady you must practise sedulously to be a delightful young one. It is worth a bit of hard work to begin with, for middle-age lasts longer than youth, and middle-

27

aged ladies who are not delightful are not anything; they simply don't count.

One little habit I advise you to cultivate, to cultivate until it becomes as natural and as spontaneous as eating peas with a fork; it is the habit of saying "Thank you" for minor services rendered. We are all of us taught that in the nursery, I know, but an uncountable number of us, or rather of you, seem to forget it when you lengthen your skirts. Let me tell you something that happened only yesterday. I went up to Charing Cross by a mid-day train from here. The only other person in the carriage was a woman. She was a lady—you know what I mean—the sort of woman who lives in a hundred-a-year house, who keeps three maidservants and a boot boy, possibly a carriage, and who goes for a month or six weeks to the Continent or elsewhere every autumn with her husband. The sort of person who when she gives a small dinner party has little pink shades over the candles and at least two sorts of wine. I think, by the way, she was the sort who would call a table napkin a serviette, but perhaps I'm prejudiced by what happened. Well, when she reached Blackheath she rose to leave the carriage. I was sitting in the corner by the door through which she had to get out, and, of course, I opened it for her. If you sit by the door you have to open it for all the outgoers. It is a nuisance, but it has its compensation in the extra comfort of the corner seat. This woman did not say "Thank you"; she passed me without even an inclination of her sulky head. Presently two other women got in, two women of the same social standing as the one who had left. At Lewisham one of these got out. I opened the door for her. She didn't say "Thank you." At London Bridge precisely the same thing happened with the remaining third. All the way thence I meditated on writing a stinging letter to the Times on "The Decadence of Manners in the Upper Middle Class," but you who know me know that the letter is still to write. What happened psychologically to me was this: that I felt just a trifle less regard and respect for your sex, Alexa, than I was conscious of when I left home. I daresay it was unreasonable of me, but there it was. Women of our class are not really nice, I found myself saying to myself, not really and truly nice in the innermost soul of them. No wonder they don't get on with their servants, I thought to myself, for if they are rude to their social equals, what must they be to those whom they think their inferiors? I rather hated your sex for about twenty-five minutes. And please don't tell me that these impolite hussies were exceptions, because on the balance of probabilities it is most unlikely that I should have struck three exceptions in the course of one short train journey. No, Alexa, you are very rude. You are attractive sometimes, I admit; you are even, in passing moments of folly and madness, bewitching, but you are very rude. I don't mean you personally, of course, but you regarded collectively — you women, you!

I find myself getting cross even now as I write when I recall that incident, getting cross and asking myself all sorts of questions which it were well for women that men should not ask. As, for instance: Why do we put up so tamely with so much of your cheek? Cheek is a slang word, but made venerable by long use, and I can think of no other so exactly adequate, so comprehensively expressive. Why do we not give you more severe talkings to than we do? They would do you no end of good, and we know it, and yet refrain. You scarcely ever get a severe talking to, any of you. Yesterday, after leaving Charing

Cross Station, I walked up Bond Street. I was really going somewhere, oh sceptical child; you must not think your father was merely loafing. I was not in a hurry, and I looked at the shops. There were lots of pretty women driving up and down in their carriages, but I did not look at them; I was at odds with the whole sex. Well, those shops! With the exception of a fishmonger's, a few most attractive tobacconists, in which you cannot get a briar root pipe under 25s., and a stray tailor or two, all those shops were women's shops; full of hats for women to wear, each hat to be worn about twice, or at the most half-a-dozen times; shops full of frocks, each frock costing more than a week's earnings of a man who works hard to make, say, £2000 a year; shops creaming over with fluffy, frilly under-things, the fluffiest and the frilliest of which disappear for ever when once they leave the shop, or, let us say, almost disappear. And then the jewellers! Rubies, emeralds, sapphires, opals in little heaps on velvet-lined trays. Diamonds and diamonds, and yet more diamonds flashing in the sunlight, flashing scorn and contempt upon all such as are too poor to purchase them; and gold, gold enough to have paved the street! Oh, and the pearls, the ropes, nay, rather the cables of pearls. Pearl fishing, they used to tell me in my Child's Guide to Knowledge, is a perilous profession, and a profession followed wholly by men. And all the things that these shops displayed—of course, there was more than as much again in drawers and cupboards and stout iron safes within the shops—were to be bought by men and given to women. For what? For what, in the name of reason? Men, merely as men, give to women as much as women, just as women, give to men; and so that part of the account is squared by nature's self, as it were. But all this balance, this ransack of Bond Street, of South

African and Eastern and Australasian mines, of ocean depths, of forest solitudes, all this is collared by women, and they won't even say "Thank you." It is true I did not give those three women yesterday any jewels to speak of; but still I did save them the soiling of their light-coloured gloves, and you know by experience, Alexa, that carriage door handles on our railway are always filthy.

Forgive this outburst, which, after all, so far as you are concerned, is quite impersonal, but out of the bitterness of the heart the pen writeth. You want to be, and I want you to be, an exceptional woman, and the easiest way in which to be an exceptional woman is to be a polite one. I don't think there is any radical difference between the sexes in the way of politeness. We are all born impolite—there is nothing much more impolite than a young baby—but one sex acquires politeness and the other doesn't—that's where it is. I wonder if you have ever noticed that. If not, just use your eyes for the next four-and-twenty hours, and once more you will be compelled to admit and to admire the accuracy of your father's criticisms of life. Watch, watch closely, next time you see two or three young men talking to two or three women in a drawing-room or at a garden party. Notice the difference (it is not a subtle, it is a quite blatant difference) between the attitude and tone of the men to the women and those of the women to the men. Unless the men be rank outsiders, and that sort is not likely to come your way, you will find in the men's attitude and tone a deference, a respectful diffidence—how shall I put it?—quite lacking in the women. However foolish, jejune, inconsequential be the remarks of any one of the women the man immediately talking to her will put on an air of interest; he will treat her as though anything she said had some real importance; he will receive her feeblest joke as though it were wit of the most polished. But she, well, if he doesn't amuse her she won't even try to look amused, and if he bores her she will most unmistakably look bored. It is horribly impolite to look bored, you know. To bore is beastly, but to look bored is damnable. Most women behave as though their mere existence were a blessing to men, as though all that men could possibly ask of them was just to be there! It is not enough, you know, Alexa; it really isn't, and in our saner moods we men feel that. We don't say unpleasant things of you, but we feel them.

The worst of it is that social custom accepts the woman's point of view and enforces it. Think what happened to me last week. It was on Wednesday—on Wednesday your mother and I dined with the Devrients. Your mother was all right from start to finish. She was taken down by Forsyth—I know you rather admire him, and you are right, for he is about as clever as they make them, and talks even better than he writes. But, then, your mother is a woman, and these sort of things are arranged for the likes of her and you. But I! In obedience to that monstrous social convention which pairs off married men with married women— I never felt it so bitterly before, for your friend, the beautiful Janet, was there and sat opposite me, hidden behind a tall epergne of tall flowers, and I'm fond of Janet, and you say she likes me—I was sent down with Mrs — (never mind, I won't mention names), a middle-aged woman, who has no beauty nor traces of beauty, who is neither clever nor interesting, who is nothing, so far as I could make out, but stupid and rather greedy. For the whole of that awful dinner—it lasted from eight until a quarter to ten—I had to make myself agreeable to that preposterous person. And I did it. I was as nice and kind as anything. I plied her with banalities, such as her soul (what there was of it) loved. I wouldn't have minded her not being intelligent had she been pretty. I wouldn't have minded her not being pretty had she been intelligent; but she was neither, and at the end of it I felt as though my brain had been wiped out with a sponge. Now, there was a man there with whom I particularly wanted to talk, he is one of the few men out of whom one always sets an idea or two, but devil a word could I get with him, and all because it is taken for granted that I, a man, must needs want to sit next to a woman. On the way home your mother remarked what a delightful evening it had been, and how quickly it had passed! I said—but you who know me, Alexa, know quite well that I said nothing.

The Registrar-General's returns inform me that men are marrying less freely than they used, and that each year they marry less freely than in the year before. It is almost the one piece of evidence I can discover of the growth and development of intelligence among my sex. It means, say the commentators in the newspapers and the magazines, that men are getting more selfish, more exacting. It does. As we get more and more civilised so shall we demand more and more from life. My savage ancestor asked but little here below. I ask quite a lot, and get some. My remote descendant will ask more, and get all of it. Of course, men who fall in love will continue to marry; the Registrar-General will always have them to go on with. For a man in love the mere girl suffices. But hitherto the marriage returns have been made up by the marriages of a certain number, and a pretty large number, of men who have not been in love and who consequently can see things, I mean women, more or less as they really are. For them the mere girl does not suffice. She has got to be a nice girl as well, a girl who takes as much trouble to be nice as she does, say, to be clean. These are the fellows, I feel certain, whose defection has caused, and will further cause, the fall in the marriage rate. Your sex is being found out, my child, found out at long last by mine. When the discovery is quite complete Lord only knows what sort of a world we shall have!

I don't suppose it has ever struck you before how nice we are to you—now has it?—how patient we are with your caprices, how tolerant of your tempers, how semi-blind to your deficiencies, how little and how rarely we use against you the strength, moral, mental, and physical, that is ours. An excellent French priest once advised me, as a cure for discontent, to spend half an hour three times a week in meditating upon my blessings. You do that, Alexa, and don't forget that perhaps, on the whole, the chiefest of yours is the possession of a most wise and always a most loving

Father

DRESS AND FASHION

Jan. 2, 19—.

My dear Alexa,—

Don't be alarmed at getting a letter from me not in reply to one of yours. Nothing has happened. "All is silver grey," as Andrea del Sarto says. I won't add "placid and perfect with my art" as he does, because it is cheek to call one's work perfect even when it is, but, at any rate, both I and my art are placid enough.

No, nothing has happened. That is the worst of it. When one reaches my age nothing ever does happen unless one makes it happen. When one is young adventures, excitements, thrills, come suddenly out of the void, thus adding to the ordinary joy of them the throb of the unexpected. But when one is older one has to fare forth out into the void and seek diligently adventures, excitements, thrills; and if one has one's living to earn, and a whole lot of little things to see after, why then one hasn't much time for excursions into the void.

This is a purely selfish letter. It is written to relieve my mind; by way of getting down in black and white some thoughts that have been twisting and twirling about like maggots in my brain all the afternoon. In that respect, at least, I am an artist, Alexa, and, forgive me, my daughter, in that same respect, you are not.

The artistic temperament is not, as fools of novelists appear to think, an itching to be singular or noticeable in any way, an inclination to wear ridiculous neck-ties, to omit to wash behind the ears, or to live with people to whom one is not married; and to quarrel with them. It is the desire, the invincible desire, to externalise and express in paint or pencil, in clay or marble, in musical sounds or in written words, one's emotions, one's thoughts, one's aspirations, one's dreams.

You, for instance, draw. For a girl of your years and training you draw rather well. But when you see a thing that appeals to you—a face, a landscape, a little bit of an interior, you do not ache and ache until you have got it down in pencil upon paper. You are quite content to keep it within you. I, when I get ever such a stupid idea in my head, am miserable until I see it before me in words, in words arranged as well as I know how to arrange them. I would rather, far rather, keep an aching tooth in my jaw than an aching idea in my head. And so, though my neck-ties are ever the correctest of their kind that Bond Street knows, and though I never do any of those other things peculiar to the artistic temperament of rubbishy fiction, I do claim to belong to the great company of artists.

By the way, I have often wondered what the author of the Te Deum was about not to have added another line to it:—

"The great Brotherhood of Artists, throughout all the world:
Praise Thee."

Every artist, in every bit of honest work he does, though he may not mean it or know it, praises God. How supremely well Kipling expressed the gist of our creed when he wrote in that exquisite Envoi to "Life's Handicap"; you remember it:—

"One instant's toil to Thee denied
Stands all Eternity's offence."

And now to come down from the heights to the valley—I never could breathe freely on mountain tops, Alexa; that's why I hate Switzerland so cordially. It is not the touring Anglican clergy and their impossible wives I object to so much; it is those appalling Alps. But, as I was going to say, I write this letter because I spent a whole half-hour this morning reading a woman's paper. At least, I'm not sure it called itself a woman's paper, it might have been a woman's page in an ordinary paper. I don't know where the thing has got to now, so I can't refer to it. I found it on the hall table when I came down to breakfast.

Doesn't it make you feel a good deal ashamed of your sex and of yourself, as one of it, when you come across a woman's page in a newspaper? Doesn't it make you feel pretty much as you would feel if you saw someone of your own standing behaving rudely at dinner? or being impolite to a child? Don't you ask yourself, with something as near to a swear word as you can get, "Whom on earth is all the rest of the paper for then? Are women so small, so narrow, such children, such idiots as to have no interest in politics, in art, in science, in literature; in all the extraordinary doings of human beings all over the world, such as the rest of the paper discusses and records?"

"The Women's Corner!" Think of it, Alexa, child of my heart! The corner into which the poor stunted, shrivelled, petty-minded creature must betake herself to read about dress. Pah!

Here your feminine intuition will tell you that I am in rather a bad temper. There, there, I don't mean to sneer at feminine intuition. Heaven knows I have both profited and suffered from it enough, and more than enough in my time, and when the sum comes to be cast up it will be found, I daresay, that I have profited as much as I have suffered.

But I am in rather a bad temper with that woman's paper, not because it was all about dress, but because it was all wrong about dress. I don't mean wrong in the absurd details—I know nothing of them—but wrong in the essence, wrong in the soul of it.

Here anyone but you would say "What in the world does the man mean by talking about soul in an article on dress?" You won't say it because you know—we have agreed about it often—that an article on anything whatever that has no soul in it, is not an article at all; it is just a bladder of rattling peas.

It is not because I despise or even think lightly of dress, that I am so unwontedly annoyed with the person who wrote all this slops. On the contrary, it is because I am fulfilled with the idea of the importance of dress and of the part it plays in the amenities and pleasures of life. You have often told me after we have been out together, or people have been here, and I have been admiring this lady or that, that I did not even know what she had on. Precisely. That was because she was well-dressed. Had she been badly dressed I should have known fast enough. The woman is well-dressed of whose costume you remember only the ensemble, what we artists call the total impression—an impression of colour and contour. Or sometimes of nothing even so definite as that, of fluffiness merely.

Now the writer of all this abominable fustian knew nothing of that, that elementary philosophy of dress. He, she, it—I don't know what the sex of the creature was—thought all of the costume and nothing of the woman. With him, her, it, the woman was a thing to be worn with a costume, not the costume a thing for a woman to wear. You do see the tremendous difference, don't you? But, of course, you do.

Really—but there, one must be tolerant. These people are flatly ignorant, and, moreover, they are the hirelings of others whose business it is to make money out of dress. That, nowadays, at anyrate, is the meaning of fashion in the restricted sense of the word. Fashion is not a mode of being beautiful or even of changing from one variety of beauty to another, or of changing to meet changing circumstances. It is a means of putting money into the pockets of dressmakers and manufacturers. These people are getting stronger and stronger, more and more arrogant.

Take a case in point. Once upon a time, not so long ago, every woman in our class had what was called "a set" of furs. It was horribly expensive to begin with, but it was taken care of and it lasted, oh, I don't know how long. Of course, that didn't suit the furriers and fur sellers—the fierce competition of commerce and all the silly rest of it—and so, though the wearing of furs is still the comfortable fashion, each season sees a change in the smaller fashion of the furs, the cut of them, the kind, and so on, and the women even in our class, who don't adopt the latest thing, feel hopelessly uncomfortable and out of it. They either go cold, or wear cat-skin or rabbit-skin faked to look like something expensive, or spend money that they haven't got.

With that rabbit-skin and cat-skin I have struck the note of fashion as it is in the suburbs, the provinces, and everywhere else except among the rich and idle people to whom money does not matter, the people who do nothing to make money, and so have most of it to spend. The designers for the big dressmakers design something that is perhaps, though by no means certainly, beautiful enough. If perchance it be beautiful, its beauty lives in the artistry and science of its fashioning, and the material of which it is made. Now the people at the top can purchase, without feeling it, the artistry, the science, the rare and costly material. But the others, you see, can't.

Nevertheless, pricked and spurred by the low-down fashion journalists, they feel that life is a desert without the new thing in some shape or another. So they get it inartistically designed, unscientifically cut, and of some cheaper, commoner stuff. Result, they don't look a bit like Duchesses after all, but only like what they are, silly and snobby women. These are hard words, Alexa, but I am cross to-day.

Fashion in its smaller sense, "the fashion" as it is forced upon women by the dressmakers and designers, as a card is forced by a sharper on a flat, is for nine people out of ten an accursed thing, a monstrous thing. It assumes that all women will look well dressed in the same way. Now, if anything is certain, it is that of any hundred women selected haphazard, not more than ten can dress in the same way and look anything but ridiculous. The human body is, as you learnt when you used to draw it at the Slade and at Colorossi's, a subtle thing, and demands the subtlest treatment. There are idiosyncrasies of body as there are of mind. I don't mean merely that some women are tall, some short, some thick, and others thin, some curvy and others angular. That has to be remembered, too, but I mean something more elusive than that.

Let us take a concrete case. You are not very different in height or form from your friend, Berta Roselli. You are not a bit prettier. A person just looking casually at you two—a second-rate milliner sort of person—would say that the same sort of costume would suit you both equally well. Yet how delightful you used to look in those frocks which you call, I think, "Princess" frocks, and how completely they took away the delightfulness from Berta. I told her so once in so many words when we were walking round the garden together, and she had the good sense never to wear them again. If you ask me why they enhanced your charm, and destroyed Berta's, I can't tell you. Perhaps there is no "why."

Then again, colour. It drives the artistic soul furious to be told that "heliotrope is to be fashionable in the approaching season," because one knows at once what one is in for. Think of heliotrope or of any other colour or tint in the universe worn beside every sort of complexion, with every sort of shade of hair! It makes one's nerves stand on end like quills. There again, the rich women score because they can, and do, change their complexions and their hair to "match," as this putrid paper calls it, the fashionable colour. The poorer women try to do the same thing, and look—well. Or don't even try, and then!—

This is merely a grumbling letter, not a didactic essay, and so I will offer no advice in it. To offer advice one should be in a judicial mood, serene, detached! but I may just say this. The one fatal thing in dress is to wear anything because you happened to have admired it on someone else, and for that reason only. The one triumphant thing in the matter of dress is to remember that you are yourself and not that other person. In all other matters women seem to remember it easily enough. In the matter of dress only do they lose their sense of identity.

Now, Alexa, turn on me, do, and riposte by telling me that men are every bit as bad; that they too are the slaves of fashion. Say things about my waistcoats if you like; I don't care, for I have a crushing retort up my sleeve. Think of the things that tailor people have tried to force upon us and how miserably they have failed; how they have tried to make us go back to peg-tops, to wear coloured coats and knee-breeches, as evening dress. Think of these things and withhold the gibe. Or, don't. I do not mind. Sedate in my sense of my sex's immeasurable superiority,

I remain,
Your angry and aesthetic
Father

A MORAL QUESTION

Jan. 15, 19—.

My dear Alexa,—

Your last letter interested and amused me vastly, as I know you intended it should. It is much the best thing in the way of writing you have ever done. I read and re-read and read it yet again after breakfast, and then I carefully, though regretfully, burnt it. One can spare oneself and others a lot of unhappiness by the simple process of burning letters, especially women's letters, more especially still charming women's charming letters. Indeed, the more charming the woman and the more charming the letter the more urgently do the flames clamour for their rights of destruction. Had anyone else read this last letter of yours, say, ten years hence, they would have formed an entirely false impression of you, and had even you read it yourself after that lapse of time you would have formed almost as false an impression of yourself. Almost, I say, not quite, for you, I fain hope, would remember the sort of man to whom it was written. And it is the character of the recipient even more than that of the writer which gives the keynote of every letter worth the reading. An intimate letter is the achievement of two personalities—it is a kind of dialogue in which one of the interlocutors is silent, or rather, is heard only by the other. That is why published letters nearly always lack interest; we do not hear that other.

Now, if anyone but your understanding father had read that last letter of yours, they would have thought you "not quite a nice girl" to have repeated little bits of scandal which you have picked up in a house in which you are a welcome guest, and to have criticised so freely your hosts and their friends. They would have liked the letter, mind you—they would have chortled over it in pharisaical glee—I chortle, too, but I chortle not as the Pharisees chortle—but they would not have liked you, for they would have feared and distrusted you, as critics are always distrusted and feared by the stodgy, especially critics of life. They, you see, these hypothetical but now impossible readers of your letter, would not have known me—would not have known, as you do, that I enjoy scandal and appreciate criticism; and would therefore have failed to realise how dutiful a daughter you were in giving me the things I like.

Need I, to a girl of your perceptiveness, attempt to justify the enjoyment of scandal? Surely it is the exceptional, not the ordinary, which should and does interest us. If, for instance, one were to discover a pork butcher, who spent all the daylight hours in butchering pork, witching the midnight with an exquisite performance of Bach's Chaconne on a Strad, one would be interested in the man, not because he was a pork butcher, but because he was a virtuoso who loved Bach and possessed a Strad. If Dr. Clifford were caught with a guitar serenading a lady's maid in Gower Street, how one's interest in the man would spring to life—how much of his windy rhetoric would instantly be forgotten? One side of our heads would condemn him, no doubt, but how the whole of our hearts would warm to the man? Ah, that one touch of nature! Forgive the banal quotation, but I don't often quote from other people's works, do I? Well, then, scandal is interesting because it is exceptional. And conduct that is not exceptional is not scandal. No one would call the improprieties of Messalina scandals; they were just the commonplace occurrences of her daily life. Now, these four persons of whose doings you tell me are made interesting to me now by the very fact that I have always held them to be of the properest sect of the proper. Next time I meet Mrs — (I had better omit the name) I shall look at her from an entirely different point of view. I shall make an effort to talk to the woman, whereas, as you know, last time I took her down to dinner I devoted myself in esurient silence to the entrées. See now, my daughter, what a kindly act you have done her in repeating that little morsel of scandal. For, as you know, when I do try to talk—really to talk—I generally succeed rather well. You have assured the dear and erring lady at least one pleasant dinner party.

But you ask me—or seem to ask me, though you do not put your query in so many words, what ought to be your own attitude to the lady in question—should you continue "to know" her, as the phrase goes, in the future. Of course, you can't help knowing her just now, for a guest must needs be courteous to fellow guests, or leave the host's house as quickly as is compatible with politeness. Very well, Alexa, let us go into this matter for a moment. What do we, you and I, know of this lady, "know for certain," as the phrase goes? We know her to be a kindly if not an obtrusively intelligent person. We know, if you come to think of it, quite a lot of nice, kind things she has done for other people, things she might have left undone and caused no remark, superfluously kind things, that is. We know her to be— for we have seen her in her own home—a devoted and efficient mother—alas that the two terms should not be synonymous—to her little children. Judging by her husband's conduct to her, he finds her an eminently satisfactory wife. Personally, though I have never heard her say a brilliant or even a clever thing, I have never heard her say an unkind one. As to this other matter of which you tell me, we are not quite sure that it is true, are we? A thing that is neither confessed nor proved is doubtful, and according to the wholesome custom of English law—and English law, broadly speaking, is English common sense—the accused has always the benefit of the doubt. But, you seem to hint, you yourself are "morally certain" that it is true. Moral certainties lead often to immoral judgments, Alexa, and, like moral victories, are always eminently unsatisfying. But let us take it for granted that it is true. What then? It is assuredly nothing that immediately concerns you or your relations with the woman, is it? You do not catch yourself desiring to follow her example in any way, do you? You find no trace of her backslidings in her conversations with you? So far as you can perceive, and you have pretty sharp eyes, my daughter, it does not affect her life or manners in any way whatever. You told me you know, that it came upon you as an overwhelming surprise. You may reply that such a thing "must" in some way affect a woman's life. I reply that it is not with what must, but with what does perceptibly happen that we in this practical work-a-day world only are concerned. We do well to leave musts to the hereafter.

In asking yourself whether you shall or shall not continue "to know" this lady, you are really and essentially asking yourself whether you shall act as judge, jury and executioner to a person accused of an offence against current convention, or, yes, if you like, against current morality. But I would point out to you that even in Law, which is at best but a rough and ready attempt to secure justice, the peculiar facts of the offence, the temptations that led up to it, are taken into some sort of account. The plea of extenuating circumstances has weight. Moreover, the accused is allowed to speak in his defence either by his own lips or those of skilled counsel. Now your court, the court which you in secret hold, and where you alone are judge, jury, prosecutor, and witnesses—your court knows nothing, and can know nothing, of peculiar facts, and of special temptations—it can mitigate nothing on account of extenuating circumstances, because it is wholly ignorant of their existence or non-existence. The accused's lips are sealed, and there is no counsel to plead for her. Do you think, then, that a court so constituted is at all likely to get anywhere near to justice in its decisions? How would you like to be tried, and executed, by such a court, if you were charged with stealing a yard of ribbon?

You may reply, and I think you will, for you are a persistent little dialectician when you like, that an analogy is not an argument. And, besides, that in talking of "execution" I exaggerate: that anything so unimportant a person as yourself may do can matter but little to the lady. No, perhaps not, but it matters a good deal to you, child, and it is you with whom I am concerned. An unjust act hurts the doer, hurts especially if it be a stupidly unjust act. After it he will be a trifle stupider, blunter, more prejudiced than he was before. There is nothing roots itself—no, not even the horse-radish in our garden—so easily, and is so hard to eradicate, as prejudice. Now prejudiced and strong you may be, my child, but you can't be prejudiced and delightful, and, as I have so often told you, above all things I want you to be delightful.

So far you are delightful, and you are strong, too, and it is because you are strong that I am going to say one thing more on this matter. The moral code of society is not equally valid in all its clauses. Some are of more importance and significance than others. Those which say we must not murder and we must not steal are of immeasurable importance, because they apply not to this time or that, or to that place or this, but to all times and to every place. A society which permitted or winked to any extent at murder or theft would cease, almost at once, to be a society. We are here now living in comparative comfort and security because societies in the past forbade murder and theft; therefore the commands which treat of these offences are of what we philosophical old buffers call universal validity. But there are other commandments in the moral code of the day which are only "of the day," as it were. Time was when they were not—places are where they are not, and possibly time will come again when they will not be. The morality which they seek to maintain is never more than the morality of a phase in human evolution. It may be valid for that phase, but it has not universal validity. Now, judgments and actions based on universal validity must needs be ever so much more assured than judgments and actions based on phasal validity, if you will allow the phrase to pass. Don't misunderstand me. I don't want to minimise the importance of the rules and regulations which are "only of the day," for, after all, that day is the day in which we live. Still, you see there is a difference, isn't there? Yes, and it is just one of those differences of which a wise and delightful young woman should take count.

Of course, I have not nearly exhausted my subject, but I have very nearly exhausted myself, and
I am your tired
Father

THE LIMITS OF FLIRTATION

Feb. 20, 19—.

My dear Alexa,—

What a very short note! Its brevity and its interrogativeness give it almost the urgency of a telegram. And yet how am I to answer it, how am I even to begin to answer it in less than half a dozen pages of quarto?

I will not remind you of the old saying that a certain sort of person can ask more questions in five minutes than a wise man can answer in a lifetime. I will not remind you, I say, because you are not the sort of person the old saying means, and I feel sure that when you asked your question you did not do it just to annoy, but because for some reason or another you really wanted to know. Was it personal, that reason? Because, if so, I think, perhaps, on the whole you had better come home.

What, you ask me, are the limits of flirtation? Where does it begin; where end?

I wish you hadn't used the word: it is a word I happen intensely to dislike, to dislike with one of those prejudices of which we can never give a satisfactory account. I think, perhaps, I dislike it because it always brings before me a mental image of one of my own sex making a fool or a rogue of himself. And yet I cannot blame you, for I myself have been quite unable to find a synonym for it.

"Coquetry" is a pretty word, but coquetry, I quite recognise, is a different thing. Coquetry is exclusively feminine. Now it takes two to make a flirtation, and one of them must not be a woman. And then, after all, the word has a worthy ancestry.

Do you know who invented it? A dozen pairs of gloves to one you don't? It was that greatest of all gentlemen that ever were, Lord Chesterfield, and he, like the gallant fellow he was, modestly attributed it to some unnamed lady of his acquaintance.

I came across it quite a little while ago in Volume XVI. of my British Essayists. You know them, those little books bound in expensive calf with red labels, which nearly fill a whole bookshelf in the library, and which you always refuse to open because you say they look so dull. Well, in No. 101 of The World, dated December 5, 1754, Lord Chesterfield is praising your sex for the good service it has done to the English tongue; and I can't think how he could! "I never see a pretty mouth opening to speak," he says, "but I expect, and am seldom disappointed, some new improvement of our language."

Happy times! Happy man! If only he could have been here the other day when the Darkleigh girls called. Their entire vocabulary consisted of one word, "ripping." No, I do them wrong. There was another, "rag." And yet what an extremely charming girl Muriel is, isn't she? And, after all, why should a woman be a dictionary?

But to return to Lord Chesterfield. He goes on to say: —

"I assisted at the birth of that most significant word

'flirtation,' which dropped from the most beautiful mouth in the world, and which has since received the sanction of our most accurate Laureate in one of his comedies. Some inattentive and undiscerning people have, I know, taken it to be a term synonymous with coquetry; but I lay hold of this opportunity to undeceive them, and eventually to inform Mr Johnson that flirtation is short of coquetry and intimates only the first hints of approximation, which subsequent coquetry may reduce to those preliminary articles that commonly end in a definitive treaty."

I have quoted Chesterfield merely for the sake of historic interest, not because his definition is much to the point just now. Since his time the word flirtation has changed its meaning, just as the thing has changed its character. It means a good deal more to-day than those "first hints of approximation." Flirtation with us does not end (except by some calamitous accident) in the "definitive treaty" of marriage. The proof of which is that when it does we usually say, or think, "Oh, then it wasn't a flirtation after all, it was serious;" implying, of course, that that which is serious is not flirtation.

Not but what stupid people among us misuse the word abominably. You will sometimes hear a woman accused of flirting with a man when she has been merely making herself as delightful as she knows how to him; doing her simple duty to herself and to him, that is.

But we need not trouble ourselves, you and I, as to what stupid people say or think. We agreed that we wouldn't, a long time ago, you remember. I have noticed, too, that people who say things about us always are stupid—which is one to us, isn't it?

No, no, flirtation to-day may go a long way beyond those first hints of approximation and still remain flirtation, without reaching those limits you talk of. It may ... but perhaps only concrete instances have value in a discussion of this sort, so let me give you one. A day or two ago, I went, rather late in the afternoon, to the Exhibition of Old Masters now on in Burlington House. I wish you had been there too; there is gorgeous Sir Joshua, which you would have knelt down and worshipped. I should have done it myself but for a sense of humour and a touch of rheumatism in the knee. Well, in the water-colour gallery I came upon a man I know and you know, with a woman I know and so do you. They were not looking at the drawings, they were sitting on a seat between two screens. My almost feminine intuition (don't jeer) told me that they had not looked at a picture since they had passed the turnstile. However, please understand, Alexa, that there was not the slightest harm in those two people being where they were on that afternoon.

At our time of day and amongst our set, I should hope, any man might go to any picture gallery with any woman and escape censure. But the point about these two people was this. When they saw me, and saw that I saw them, they seemed embarrassed. And then the man gave me a look which meant, if ever a look meant anything, "I know you're a decent chap, and I am confident you will hold your tongue," and the lady did not look at me at all, she fidgeted with the edge of her veil. The veil, by the way, of course, gave the whole thing away. It was thickish. People who want to see pictures don't wear thick veils.

Now, that embarrassment, that look of the man's at me, that little nervous gesture of the lady's, told me that here was a flirtation. Nothing more than a flirtation so far. I am confident of that. But a flirtation, mind you, that had almost reached the limits.

An understanding, a secret understanding, an understanding from which the rest of the world is excluded, is of the very essence of flirtation. The entente, the agreement, may never have been made by words spoken in corners, or written in notes, but it must at least have been made in looks or, no, perhaps not by anything so definite as they, by the creation of that most impalpable but most real thing, an atmosphere, an emotional atmosphere.

When does a flirtation begin, then? It begins directly she has succeeded in convincing him (of course you may reverse the sexes) that he is more attractive to her than any of the other men about. Mind, I say in convincing him. Until he is convinced the thing has not begun; it is only an attempt at a flirtation—and to fail in such an attempt is, with one exception, the most disastrous defeat a woman can sustain. No woman can encounter two beatings of that sort and retain her self-esteem. Her amour propre is irreparably ruined. A man, on the other hand, can survive any number of rebuffs and come up smiling to face the next; for he can always comfort himself with the thought that it was the lady's prudence and not his own unattractiveness that was responsible for the licking.

A flirtation must be without serious intent. If one of the parties to it have anything more definite in view, consciously in view, then he or she is not flirting; it is a one-sided affair. It is in no way destructive of the accuracy of my definition that most affairs are one-sided affairs.

There may be in a flirtation, there nearly always is, a sort of subtle subconsciousness of delightful possibilities, of dangerously delightful possibilities, but that is all there may be; and it is just these vague possibilities that give the salt to the dish.

Flirtation then you see, Alexa, is, like virtue, its own reward. That, I think, is the only respect in which it does resemble virtue. Like art, it must exist only for its own sake; and it is remarkably like art. Indeed, it is no inconsiderable part of the art of life. The object of art, as Pater says somewhere, is to render radiant, to intensify, our moments. That and nothing else is the object, so far as it has an object, of flirtation.

Of course it gratifies our vanity, and of all gratifications, or nearly all, the gratification of vanity is the sweetest, the one with least alloy or unpleasant after-taste. Vanity suffers from hunger, but never from indigestion, no, nor from satiety. There are few things in this world which give a man, who is a man and not a pudding, such a tingling thrill of pleasure as the consciousness that a woman, an ordinarily discreet woman, has run the ever-so-slightest risk of compromising herself for his sake.

A woman once told me—quite a nice woman, Alexa, not a cat, nothing like a cat—that life's height was the knowledge that she could raise a man to the summits or cast him down to the depths, by giving or withholding a glance as she left the dinner-table for the drawing-room. So you see flirtation has its points as a form of sport.

Obviously then, as I said, there must be an understanding, a tacit, if temporary, alliance between the pair. They must have made a little circle for themselves, a little circle in which they two move alone, from which the rest of the world is excluded, as it were, by a burning bush. There may be a ménage à trois, indeed, I am told that the ménage à trois is one of the commonest of social phenomena, but a flirtation à trois there can never be. A woman may flirt with two men, or a man with two women, but neither of the two must know of the other's existence or the thing falls to pieces.

It is in truth a sort of exercise preliminary to the duel of sex. The combatants are combatants only by courtesy; they fence with the buttons on the foils. So long as the game is played according to the rules, there is likely to be naught more seriously discommoding than a scratch or a tiny little blue bruise which in a day or two will disappear. But, and here is the spice of it, at any moment one of the buttons may come off by accident, or be taken off by fraud, and then—well, then certainly a garment may be torn to rags, possibly a heart may be pierced.

Where does flirtation end? you ask. Well, I can tell you where it never ends. It never ends in a row. Never, at any rate, when he or she has more brains than a guinea-pig. Of course, with downright fools there is no telling. If there be ever so slight a row, ever so faint a scandal, then there has been something more than a flirtation. The limits have been passed; a button, somehow or other, has come off a foil. When somebody is trying to get back somebody's letters somebody has leaped the limits: be sure of that.

Miss Rhoda Broughton, an author whom young women of to-day are a little apt to slight, makes Sarah in Belinda say:—"I may be a flirt, but thank heaven in the whole length and breadth of Europe there exists not a scrap of my handwriting." Or words to this effect. May be a flirt forsooth! Of course she was a flirt, and a flirt of accomplishment, or she could never truthfully have made the boast.

But the limits? Well, they are like most other limits that determine the conduct of men and women. They are shifting limits, they change from age to age, and from climate to climate; nay, more than that, from social set to social set. Judging from what I hear on the top and bottom levels of our present society there is no fault to find with their narrowness; and even with us though they may be not so wide as a church door (horrid simile that; a church should never even be thought of in connection with a flirtation) they will do, they will serve.

Perhaps you want me to be practical though. Well, here goes then. Secret assignations should be avoided as beyond the limits, so should the underground post. You know what I mean by the underground post; letters sent to clubs or to post-offices.

Dark corners at dances? Well—yes. A dark corner may just be inside the boundary, but a clasped hand in that dark corner is well over it. But by the way, Alexa, on the whole it seems not wise in me to set out these limits for you, because the limits of flirtation are also the perilous edges of—find the word for me in the Thesaurus. There is plenty of room well within those limits for you to entertain yourself, and others, in security. Keep away from the limits, for, as I said, they are vague, apt sometimes, in emotional moments, to become blurred, invisible even perhaps. When a girl of your tender years gets near to the limits she is likely to call for the prompt and most disagreeable intervention of a, and particularly of

Your, stern and relentless,
Though never heavy,
Father

MEN'S LOVE

Jan. 20, 19—.

My dear Alexa,—

Your appetite for knowledge does you credit. It is inherited, doubtless. And how comprehensive it is! You wish you knew all about men, do you? A moderate wish; a wish that if realised would make you empress of the world. Yes, that and nothing less than that is the destiny of the woman, when she arrives, who knows all about men. We shall not see her just yet though, and when, if ever we do, then, as Swinburne's distressful lover says:

> "Content you, I shall not be there."

So as things are I sleep peacefully o' nights. That masterful lady does not even trouble my dreams.

Don't you know, child, that men are now, and always have been, combined in a conspiracy not to let women know all about them; nay, more than that, to permit women to know as little as possible? Men are not very clever in other ways, but they are, I fancy, clever enough to make that particular conspiracy a success. They have done very well so far, anyhow.

Women know curiously little about men; curiously little considering the long time they have had to study the subject, and how greatly it has always been to their interest to know as much as possible. Take women novelists, for instance—not the silly sort, but the very best of them, the giantesses of fiction— Georges Sand, George Eliot, Charlotte Brontë—to say nothing of

58

the second string, the women writers of our day, the Mrs Craigies, the Ouidas, the Mrs Humphrey Wardses. Why is it, by the way, that when there was no "Woman Movement" there were great women artists, and that now when woman is clamorous and obtrusive there are none?

But take, as I said, the big women. Scarce one of them has presented us with a real live man. Think of Charlotte Brontë's Rochester! George Eliot did better. Just now and then some of her men do really think and feel as men feel and think. But that, I suggest, was because George Eliot was herself something more or less than a woman. The men in women's novels, it is true, act as men act, but they rarely or never think as men think. Women are keenly observant; they see what men do; they don't know, because men never tell them, what men think.

Now please don't make, even in your own mind, the obvious and inept reply, "Neither do men know women," because by the universal consent of women themselves the great men novelists, and some of the small ones, have portrayed veritable women; Balzac, for example, and George Meredith, and Thomas Hardy and Flaubert! Was there ever a realer woman than Madame Bovary?—I am not sure, though, that you have made her acquaintance.

The concealment, conscious and unconscious, begins almost at the beginning. The smallest schoolboy never lets his sisters see him as he sees himself and as he is seen of his fellows. To his sisters he talks a different language even, a different language from the language of the playground, I mean. And it is well for him that he does. If he didn't, and his father caught him at it, there would be sorrow and soreness for that boy. No novelist, man or woman, has so much as begun to depict the schoolboy as he is. Kipling is nowhere near it, nor Eden Phillpotts, nor the rest. And as for Tom Brown...!

No, not only do women not know men, but they don't even know boys, and that really is queer, because women themselves are curiously like boys in many ways, and, after all, they do have a good deal to do with the bringing up of boys. But it is wonderful how much a boy manages to hide even from his mother. I don't think he does it consciously; it is the inherited instinct of his sex—the result of natural selection, probably—explainable on Darwinian principles, like most else in this world.

You see, for you know your Darwin, if a man were to let women know all about him no decently civilised woman would ever be found so fond or so foolish as to mate with him. Consequently he would never reproduce his kind—he would not be the fittest and would not survive.

Rum, isn't it? I have only just thought of it, but I am quite sure it is a discovery of vast importance—that the continuance of the race depends upon women's ignorance of men.

Let me give you an example of their colossal ignorance of boys. Mrs Bates was here the other day. You know she is an exceptionally intelligent woman, and really learned also. She had been reading some Italian psychologist's book on Love; and, judging from what she told me, that foreigner really appears to have known something about it. It seems he gave a case of a lad of fourteen who had a passion for a lady of thirty or thereabouts. And Mrs Bates asked me if such a thing were possible! I enlightened her with frankness and great wealth of detail. But I could see she didn't believe me; she thought I was talking through my hat all the time; inventing as I went on.

I don't ask you, Alexa, whence comes this new-born desire of yours to know all about men; but I warn you that I am pretty good at guessing. However, let that pass. Not only will you never know all about men, but at present, my kiddie, you don't know anything at all. Knowledge of live things is not to be got from books or plays. All you can get from books or plays is—what shall I call it? there is no one word that will do—a sort of vague and deceptive hint of the reality. That is not very well put, but it is the best I can do for the moment. Knowledge of life means knowledge of men and women, just that and naught but that, and knowledge of life can only be got by living. You can learn no more of it from books than you could learn of a country by merely studying a map. You would, of course, learn more of it in five minutes from some intelligent and talkative traveller who had been there, and who chatted freely.

Well, your father is such a traveller, and he has made a longish journey through the territory of life, a territory in which he has looked about him with the eyes of a man. Even so, he can't do much for his daughter, but he can do something, he has done something, and he will do more if time be granted him.

Bear in mind, then, when you read of love, the love of the sexes, when you hear it talked about, when you see it, apparently going on under your eyes, that this traveller towards the end of his journeyings often catches himself doubting whether there is such a thing as love of the sexes at all, whether, in short, to call the thing "love" is not to do an outrage to language and to common sense.

Of course, you can call any thing by any name you like, but you have no sort of right to call two widely and fundamentally different things by the same name. And to call the emotion I have for you, for instance, by the same name as you call the emotion a man experiences for a woman when he is "in love" with her is monstrous. The two things are dissimilar in almost every respect.

When a man and woman are infected by what some scientific French gentleman seriously declares to be the love-microbe they are, it seems to me, the victims of all sorts of curious delusions and illusions, and they are unable to analyse their own states of mind. The man feels capable of all sorts of heroism and nobility, and the woman of any amount of self-sacrifice. That feeling of theirs is sheer delusion. In point of fact they are both in a state of highly inflamed egoism. Introduce the slightest whiff of jealousy and the heroism and the self-sacrifice are converted into the lowest-down sort of meanness. At once you get base and baseless suspicions, spying, of the opening-letters and listening-outside-doors order, and often, to wind up with, cruelty and savagery more frightful than the beast's.

Well now, is the thing, this in-loveness which can be so easily transformed into devilry, worthy of the name we give to the feeling of parents for children, or friends towards one another? Yet that first thing is what is meant when one talks of the love of the sexes!

Mind you, there is no avoiding that microbe, the anti-toxin has not yet been found, and I don't mind predicting that if ever it be found the demand for it will be of the slackest. I don't mind confessing that if that microbe were swept out of the world, as we hope some day to sweep out the tubercle bacillus, the little chap would leave the world considerably duller than he found it, so dull as to be no place for the likes of me. But still we may as well see the thing for what it is. Because we are all mad sometimes, and enjoy our brief deliriums, there is no reason why in the sane intervals we should not frankly recognise what we were the last time we went mad and what we are likely to be the next.

Please don't imagine that I have written the above passage by way of a warning to you. The philosopher neither warns against the inevitable nor regrets it. He likes just to look it straight in the face sometimes, that's all. It amuses him.

But now, apart from this in-loveness—which I will not call love, hang me if I will—do men, men as a whole, men as a sex, love women, women in the lump, women as a sex? As I live, I don't believe they do! It would be interesting if some leisured and industrious person—you might take on the job, Alexa, when you return—would compile a volume of proverbs, aphorisms, epigrams, from all languages, which have women as their subject. There is scarcely one of them—I don't remember one—that has a word to say in her praise. As Dick Phenyl used to say in Sweet Lavender, ... ah heaven! a senile shudder runs through me when I think what a long time ago that was—"it's all blame, blame, nothing but blame," and a good deal more than blame, heavy vituperation, acrid snarling, and, I freely admit it, often disgusting and mendacious slander. But still, there we are; men made these proverbs and aphorisms, men cut and polished these epigrams, and men have kept them as current coin in the world.

Now I put it to you, does one satirise, ironise, slate, bully-rag, and squirt verbal vitriol at the thing one loves?

Then, watch men. You have the opportunity, since I understand you have a full house just now. Watch them, then. Do they, for instance, hurry up to the drawing-room after dinner, or do they linger down there over their wine and their talk till the hostess loses her patience and every feminine eye keeps turning to the door? No doubt if there's any man there hopelessly "in love" he would sneak up if he dared. But the others? And oh! if you were to see us the moment after the dining-room door has closed behind you, you dears! If you were to see how we draw our chairs up, to note the change in our voices, the air of comfort with which we finger our glasses, the heavy reluctance with which we rise when the host gives the word! Oh!

I suppose there's a little shooting still going on, isn't there, or is it all over? But if there is, I dare say some of the women go out with the guns, or at any rate meet the men for luncheon. Well, watch the men's faces, watch closely (don't listen to their voices, we know how to school our voices) when the women volunteer. You will see how men pant for "women's society!"

They won't have you in their clubs, Alexa; think of that. Some years ago I, greatly daring, did propose at the annual general meeting of my club that women should be admitted—to tea. I could not find a seconder. One old gentleman who, to my great surprise, did rise to second me turned out to be deaf, and thought I was proposing something quite different. That luckless attempt of mine almost ruined my reputation; the memory of it still clings to me like the traces of some fell disease. They thought I was, well—pretty much everything but what I am.

And yet how polite and altogether nice men are to you, aren't they? How promptly they spring forward to take the lightest parcel from your hand, with what lackey-like deference do they hold open the door that you may pass out! Yes, but then you are a woman, a pretty and attractive woman of their own social standing. Again I say, watch. Do they show quite the same alacrity in the case of a less delightful or of a much older woman than you? Still further, do they show any disposition at all to carry the coal-box upstairs for the housemaid—and the housemaid, after all, is a woman, you know.

No; men do not love women. Or, if they love them they love them as the hawk loves the pigeon, or as you love chocolate almonds. Men, as men, do not, I repeat, love women as women; but I love you, and I am always

Your devoted
Father

THE MAN'S POINT OF VIEW

Feb. 9, 19—.

My dear Alexa,—

No—that formal greeting inadequately expresses my emotion at the moment—I will say then, Alexa dearest—

I am really sorry that my last letter should have put you into such a flutter; should have ruffled your mind's plumage so quite unduly. I find I nearly always do come to grief in this way when I neglect the advice given me years and years ago by a wise and wicked old man, when I was a foolish and a passably good young one.

"My boy," that old rapscallion said—he was holding up a glass of his own port to the candle when he said it, and enjoying the delight of the eye previous to the pleasure of the palate. "My boy, never tell the truth to women. You'll find it infernally difficult to do any way, and it always turns out badly." He gave me much other counsel of a similar sort. Sometimes I have acted upon it and sometimes I have not. When I have I have always scored handsomely; when I haven't I have invariably been sorry for myself.

He was a remarkable old gentleman, old Gillion. He enjoyed the worst reputation of any man of his set. When I say enjoyed I mean enjoyed. He loved it; he cherished it as a collector of books cherishes his rare old editions. He died at the age of eighty-seven in an odour of diabolism, tenderly served and waited upon by a troop of affectionate and expectant grandchildren, to whom he left not a penny. Years before he had invested all his money in an annuity. But they didn't know that. They say he died with a smile on his lips. I can quite believe it. He always loved irony.

It is, as that sage reprobate said, infernally difficult to tell the truth to women, and that, I make no doubt, is why it so seldom gets told. For one thing the truth, the bare truth, is nearly always unpleasant, and so you see, the temptation to lie attacks us on our softer, our more kindly, side. I am quite sure that nine times out of ten when men deceive women they do it much less for their own sakes than for the sakes of the women. Now, don't raise your eyebrows and draw down your lip-corners, because that really is so. Moreover, they often feel (if they be of a philosophic cast they know) that the deception comes nearer to the truth than the actual bald fact would be. Bald facts are seldom or never true facts. Truth is ever a thing of atmosphere, of light and shade, of fine gradations. Truth is a point of view, sometimes a very temporary and transient point of view.

A point of view. Yes, that's it. And that is why it is not only difficult but, I incline to think, impossible for men to tell the truth to women. Suppose you have two persons whose eyes are so constructed that they can only see the world through glasses, and suppose one of these persons is doomed always to wear green glasses and the other pink glasses. How on earth can any object ever look the same to both? A can tell B that a sheet of paper is green, but he may say so for ever, and yet B will always see it pink. And the fun of the thing is that it is really white all the time! And what do I mean by "really"? I don't know.

But are men and women so different as all that, you will be asking yourself. Yes, they are. Quite as different as all that, and more so. They are wonderfully different. The longer I live and the more I look about me the greater and more distinct do the differences seem to become. I know it's the fashion just now, especially among strong women and weak men, to deny this, and to declare that as we evolve we grow nearer to, more like, each other. Sheer nonsense, my dear, sheer nonsense!

One of the most notable marks of civilisation is the way in which it differentiates the sexes. A savage father is much nearer to his daughter than I am to you. I am rather sorry for it, but it can't be helped, and this letter of yours goes some way towards proving it. And yet I don't know that I am quite honest in saying that I am sorry for it—another instance of how difficult it is to tell the truth, you see—for it seems to me that a good deal of the joy, or at any rate of the excitement, of life is brought about by just that difference. Life has little that is exciting to your civilised man, and if you deprive him of that...!

But to come to your letter. You say that I picture the world to you, the world of men and women, as a place full of ravening beasts of prey, and you add that now whenever two or three men are fluffing round you, you will feel like a defenceless pigeon surrounded by hungry hawks. Well, if my letter has done that for you it must have wrought a transformation indeed. I have seen you more than once with two or three young men fluffing (I like that word fluffing, it is apt; keep it for future use) round you and somehow it never struck me that they in the faintest degree resembled hawks or that there was anything of the silly pigeon about my daughter. They generally, I seem to remember, looked nervous and rather scared, though genuinely anxious to please, very unhawk like; but then they were young, and I dare say a callow hawk is pretty well as timid as a newly hatched chick. Courage comes with age, with the hardening of the beak and the sharpening of the talons.

Yet I am not altogether sorry if my last letter brought to you some realisation of some part of the truth; one aspect of it, let us say. Looked at from one point of view, the world of men and women is full of ravening beasts of prey. But take up another standpoint and you will see that the powers and opportunities of the beasts are often pretty narrowly limited. Limited sometimes by their own ignorance of their own powers, limited always by the social institutions which they themselves have established. It seems rum, but the wolf has filed his own fangs, the hawk has clipped his own claws.

You may be a pigeon, Alexa, but, thanks to many things, you are not a defenceless pigeon. You are defended, for instance, by your own brains, by the knowledge which I have taken good care should be yours, by the customs of the social circle in which you were born, by the institution of marriage, and most of all by the jealousy and suspicion the wolves and hawks have of one another. So on the whole you are tolerably safe, my birdie; you need not flutter a feather. Remember what I once told you in another letter when I was employing a slightly different set of metaphors—it is always the traitor in the citadel who gives the fortress away.

"If men don't really love women, women as a sex, as distinguished from their own particular women," you ask, "why is it that they protect them to such an extent, to such a so often unnecessary and troublesome extent? Why do they always rescue them first in shipwrecks and fires, and so on?"

Curiously enough, that was almost exactly the question your friend Stella put to me only yesterday when she called here at tea time and everybody but I was out.

By the way, what a ferociously advanced young woman Stella is becoming! She quite scared me now and then. I never felt at all sure what she was going to say next. She was in a great rage with one of her young men cousins who had taken her to the theatre the night before, or the night before that. I forget for the moment what the play was, but it doesn't matter. She liked it and was intensely interested in it, but the young man violently disapproved of it—disapproved of it for her, that is. Half way through the second act he insisted on her leaving the theatre there and then. Stella made a fight of it, but she couldn't make a scene, and so she caved in, and now she swears she will never speak to him again.

The reason he gave her was that he could not bear the idea of his cousin ("his cousin," you should have heard Stella emphasise the possessive) listening to such a grossly improper thing as that. Stella's very pretty face wrinkled with wrath when she told me. "His cousin," she repeated. "As though I were his property. But that's always the way with men. The man's point of view! How I hate it! They can't bear that anything of which they disapprove should come near any woman connected with them. They don't mind about the others."

And so, quite against my own will, I was compelled—the while I soothed her with chocolates—to defend, or rather to explain (it comes to the same thing) the Man's Point of View. My explanation will go some way to answering you.

Stella was right in one thing. She put her finger—what beautiful hands the girl has, by the way, did you ever notice them?—directly on the spot. It is the sense of proprietorship that does it. Men do not love women as women, but they do love, or at any rate have some sort of feeling which serves the purpose of love, their own women kind, the women "connected with them." There is nothing a bit noble in it to begin with, it is just sheer egoism; the same sort of feeling that makes a child before it can talk hold on tight to a toy that you try to take away from it. I remember you, when you were in your cradle, punched me with one fist while you clung on with the other to a woolly red ball that you would cram into your mouth. Well, just so, but more effectively would I punch a man who tried to take you away from me. And at the root the motive for the punching would be the same. So, Alexa, unless the man be quite of the right sort let him look to himself, for I still keep my punching muscles in trim.

No, in this sense of ownership there is nothing noble, nothing magnificent, nothing to swagger about. But just as a very lovely and exquisite flower may have a very dirty and ugly root, so from this sense of ownership has grown the fine flower of chivalry and the less fine and flowerlike but, for work-a-day purposes, the much more useful plant of men's protective attitude to all women, or, not to exaggerate, to a good many women.

It is sometimes inconvenient to the women concerned, no doubt, as it was the other night to Stella; but it is thanks to it that they have any sort of a time in the world. That feeling of proprietorship which a man concentrates on his own women folk he extends in a diluted and attenuated form to the women

71

of his own class, and in a form still more attenuated (sometimes very thin indeed) to all women. Roughly put it amounts to this, that each man is ready to protect any woman against any other man. There are occasions, spite of the proverb to the contrary, when hawks do peck out other hawks' eyes.

So you see on the whole it is a little ungrateful to grumble at the Man's Point of View, isn't it?

I think I said a page or two back that one of your defences was the institution of marriage. Perhaps, lest you should think I was talking mere conventional rubbish, I had better explain what I meant.

Men are not cowards; lots of them love and choose danger for its own sake. Bernard Shaw is quite wrong when he says in one of his plays that fear is the greatest of all human forces. That remark is only a little feat of intellectual gymnastics, designed to startle. But, valiant and daring blades though men are, there is one thing that they fear with a craven, shrinking, shivering terror. That thing is marriage.

"They marry!" you reply. Why, yes, and so also do they die, though often with somewhat less reluctance; and they marry just as they die, because they can't help themselves. The impulse to marriage (as things are) is as irresistible as the spear-thrust of Death. It would be interesting if in the vestry after the ceremony one could apply some species of Chinese torture to every bridegroom and extort from him the truth as to whether he did indeed want to marry this woman. He wanted this woman, of course, but did he want, actually want, to take upon himself the life-long responsibilities, the life-long expenses, the life-long risks, the life-long limitation of liberty?

Why the fact, this deep aversion of the man from marriage, this recoil from the altar, is marked in common speech, and anything that is marked in common speech "is so," as the Americans say. Don't you often hear it said that Miss So-and-So has "caught," "hooked," "captured," young Thingamy? When do you ever hear that a man has caught, hooked, or captured (in a matrimonial sense) a woman?

The institution of marriage is the highest and the stoutest barrier between the sexes that society has ever set up. That is not a paradox. It is a plain, almost an obvious truth. Thus the pigeon (poor little pigeon!) escapes many attacks from the hawks without the trouble of moving a wing. In other words, a woman meets with far fewer advances, much less pursuit, and consequently much less temptation, from men than she would were it not for this institution of marriage. The boldest and most hungry hawk thinks twice before swooping on the pigeon if he knows that the pigeon, harmless as she looks, may turn and manacle him to her for the rest of his natural life, before he knows where he is.

And so, Alexa, if you sometimes feel that fewer young men fluff around you than your many attractions might warrant, don't be depressed or self-distrustful. It is not because you are not pretty or fascinating enough; it is because they are afraid you might marry them. Their self-restraint is really the highest compliment they can pay you.

Good-bye, and don't be offended with your truth-loving
Father

THE DOMESTIC HEARTH

March 1, 19—.

My dear Alexa,—

If you have a fault—and far be it from your adoring father to suggest that you have—but if you have a fault, it shows itself in your trick of asking questions beginning with an "ought." I think my recollection is right when it tells me that your last three letters have, together with a good deal that was both interesting and diverting, contained a query as to whether you or somebody else "ought" or "ought" not to do something or other. When it is a case of You, I feel myself more or less competent to answer; for about You I do know a little, you see; but when you ask me what somebody else ought to do or to leave undone, somebody else of whom I know nothing, why, then I am stricken with a feeling of hopeless futility. I sit here and dither, and cover sheets of letter paper with my illegible handwriting only to tear them up after a miserable half-hour's boggling. For to know what a person "ought" to do, one must know the person, you see, and the circumstances in which that person is posed. There are no "oughts" unrelated to particular persons and particular circumstances. If there were, what plain sailing life's perilous voyage would be, wouldn't it? In point of dismal fact that voyage is made upon an uncharted sea. A few plain general instructions in the principles of navigation are all we get; we have to look out for the rocks and shoals and whirlpools and adverse currents for ourselves.

There are not nearly so many "oughts" in life as you in the

solemn ingenuousness of your youth doubtless imagine. As you grow older you will find the "oughts" diminish and the "musts" increase. That is to say what looks like moral freedom gradually, and not so very gradually either, gives way to what in stern fact is practical necessity. But I suppose I must come to the point.

"Ought girls to earn their own livings?" you ask in a postscript, which I can't help wishing you had forgotten to add. There is no dodging a postscript, there is no pretending one hasn't noticed it. That is perhaps why women are so fond of it. But—no longer to dodge yours—see how the facts of life limit the scope of your question. See how your "ought" is, for the vast majority of young women, at once converted into a "must." For the vast majority of young women the question does not so much as arise. They do earn their own livings as it is, and they do it not because they ought or because they choose, but just because they must. The housemaid, for instance, who made your bed this morning, and who, I hope, dusted and put straight your room— a lengthy business, Alexa, for I know your ways—do you suppose that her action was the outcome of any moral questionings or of personal predilection? Do you suppose she did it from a high sense of duty, because she felt that something would go askew with the universe or with her own soul if she left it undone? Of course she didn't. She did it because she had to do it, to do either that or something just a trifle more objectionable, on the whole. She is probably one of a large and poor family, and as soon as she had passed the Sixth Standard, or whatever it is which the law of her country demands that she should pass, she had to go out to service. There was no "ought" about it. And those young women whom you saw in Fleet Street, at mid-day, when you were there with me, you remember, a day or two before you left home, and whose behaviour struck you as being so vulgar and objectionable! They were binders' girls; they had already been working several hours in a stuffy atmosphere, and after a quarter-of-an-hour's rollicking up and down Fleet Street, they were about to return and work several more hours. And do you think that they had decided to do all that work after mature deliberation as to the rights and wrongs of it? Of course they hadn't. It was for them that, or something infinitely worse than that, and so they chose, if they can be said to choose, that. It was a case of "must," not of "ought." And when a thing must be, there is no more reckless waste of honest time possible than that spent in discussing whether it ought to be.

Your question applies then, you see, only to a very limited number of young women. It was not a thoughtfully-framed question, Alexa. It was, if you will forgive me, a middle-class sort of question. When you wrote "girls," you were thinking of yourself and of young women in a social position similar to yours, and they are rather a small minority of the earth's inhabitants; delightful, but few, comparatively. So let me frame the question for you as you would have framed it if you had thought a little more about it, and then let's get to work upon it.

What you meant to ask was, I think, this: Ought a young woman of good education, ordinary health, stature, and capacity (whose parents can afford to keep her in idleness) to live upon their income until such time as she is asked by a nice young gentleman to come and live upon his? That is about as near as we can get to it, isn't it?

Well, even that very limited interrogative proposition is not altogether easy to tackle. One question leads always directly or indirectly to another, and so we go on asking "Why?" until we come flat up against a dead wall before which we can do nothing but gibber. In the affairs of practical life it is necessary to treat some matters as settled, and one of such matters is this:—If you receive from a person services for which you make no return, you are under an obligation to that person; and to sit quiescent under an obligation, to make no effort to get out of it, is to suffer humiliation and indignity. That, reasonably or unreasonably, is the view of every decently honest man and woman, of every man and woman whose hand you would care to take in friendship. That is your own view, Alexa, when you come to think of it, isn't it? I have noticed that whenever a friend makes you a present you begin to cast about for some way in which you can make some return without doing it too obviously. Moreover, you would not accept a present at all from one who was not a friend. If one of your fellow-guests now, for instance, were to offer you a diamond bracelet, you would be in no end of a rage, and would probably write to me.

Now then, everybody of full age and capacity who is eating, drinking, dwelling in a house and wearing clothes, and yet doing nothing whatever to provide that food, drink, house and apparel, is suffering that humiliation and indignity of which we have just spoken. He may not be conscious of it. Obviously he is not (for there are many millions of him) conscious of it, but the fact remains. There is just one reply he can make to the charge. He can say, if he likes, "Oh, it is true I do nothing practical, material, in return for the many services which are done for me; but I consent to live. I exist beautifully. I look nice, I talk, when I take the trouble to talk, quite prettily. I wear my clothes with an air. I am an example of what a human being should be. Thus, by merely being, do I recompense the world for all the trouble it takes for me." If he does say that, then I for my part can think of no adequate rejoinder. If it be a man who talks like that, one kicks him and takes the consequences; if a woman, one (perhaps) kisses her and drops the controversy.

But that tiresome "ought" of yours which I feel buzzing round my head as I write, like a bee, and a bee with a sting, too! To deal with it properly I must assume something to start with, and so here goes. I assume this: One ought to do that which will enable one to live the happiest life attainable in one's circumstances and to develop one's capabilities to their fullest. I assume that, and if you query it, Alexa, I will wait until you return home and have a couple of hours' tête-à-tête with you in my study.

Now then, does a grown-up young woman live the happiest life attainable or develop her natural capacities to their fullest while she lives in her parents' house, dependent for every penny she spends upon her parents' bounty or caprice, acting under her parents' orders in all the great and in the most of the smaller doings of her life, and subject to her parents' rules, regulations, and discipline?

Judging from my own observation and knowledge of the way in which human nature is composed I haven't the smallest hesitation in answering "No." My observation tells me that there may be outward acquiescence, my penetration tells me no less surely that there is always hidden resentment. A thwarted desire for freedom works like poison in the blood; in the long run it sours the finest temper. It gives birth to a fire which, though it may never flame, continually smoulders; and, remember, this desire for freedom, for the power to do what we will, to go where we wish, to say what we like, subject always to the limitations of external circumstances, is inherent in every human breast. The restrictions of external circumstances we most of us accept without over much of rancour. What we do not accept, that against which we are in eternal revolt, is the restriction imposed upon us by other wills than ours. That impulsive desire to break away from pupillage, to strike out "on our own," is perhaps of all motives the most legitimate that can stir the human soul.

The Home as we so often know it, the Home which consists of father, mother, and grown-up dependent sons or daughters, or both, is not a place wherein such impulses and motives can rightly develop or have anything like free play. Such a Home is necessarily and inevitably a tyranny; at best a benevolent tyranny, at worst a tyranny in which benevolence is far to seek. Don't imagine that I have joined the cult of Mr Bernard Shaw and am about to say anything so ridiculously untrue as that the Home is the very worst institution in which to bring up a child, except the school. That is a mere paradox of Nihilism distraught. The Home, so far, is the best of all institutions in which to bring up a child—to bring up a child, mark, not to support a grown man or woman. It has its analogy in the nests of birds and the lairs of beasts; but Nature, for once in a way, is wiser than modern man. The young bird leaves the nest as soon as it is strong enough on the wing; the young tiger says good-bye to the lair on the day on which he can kill his own prey. The Home of grown-up sons and daughters who are not earning their own livings—even the happiest of such Homes—is a place of continual and constant compromise and surrender, of suppression, of restraint, of concealed (and not always concealed) resentments and silent rebellions. Just now and then maybe (for I want to avoid extremes) it may draw forth the best that is in us; but much more often it evokes the worst. It narrows even when it does not actually distort; it cripples even when it does not actually slay. And there is no help for it, Alexa. The profoundest wisdom, the sincerest love, can do little more than slightly ameliorate the essential, the immutable wrongness of the Thing, the subjection of adult will to adult will. Children of no matter what age who are dependent upon their parents economically, must needs be dependent in all else. The world is so constructed that he who pays the piper calls the tune. And it is well; for even worse than an ordered tyranny is an anarchic republic.

There is just another point. Marriages, Alexa, are not made in Heaven as some are still found to say, nor in Hell, as too many just now are apt to declare. They are made for the most part in the Home. The strongest condemnation of the grown-up Home is the enormous number of young women who marry to get away from it. In the name of my own sex I do resent and protest against that. It is hard upon us that we should be so often regarded by the Beloved as a sort of melancholy alternative to the Home. Girls, in our class at any rate, marry much more often with a view to being their own mistresses, as we say, than to being men's wives or children's mothers. And I sometimes fancy they are under no very serious illusions as to the radiant possibilities of the married state, these marrying maidens of ours. There was once a man, you know, who after several days' suffering from acute earache went out and had a tooth drawn. When he was asked why he supposed that the extraction of a sound tooth would remedy the agony of an unsound ear, he replied that he had never supposed anything of the kind. All he wanted was to change the pain, and that the dentist had done for him! A similar desire, I am sure, will alone account for some recent marriages of your young friends which have caused you so much puzzlement. "I cannot make out what she saw in him," you have more than once remarked to me. Well, she saw just that—a change in the pain. Not nice for him, is it? Nor so very nice for her.

And now I wonder whether you consider that I have answered your question at all satisfactorily. I daresay not, for this world is a welter, and the wisest of us is bemazed with doubts. It is possible to have doubts about everything—at least I should say about everything but one, and that is that I am always, my own kiddie,

Your loving
Father

THE TREE OF KNOWLEDGE

April 2, 19—.

My dear Alexa,—

The question put in the last paragraph of your last letter, to which I have perhaps been a little overlong in replying, is one which I should have thought I had already answered, answered, too, in the only way in which such questions can be answered satisfactorily—by actual practice. You know me well enough, I take it, to know that, like every other decently-honest man, when I have a conviction I act upon it. Mind, I say a conviction, not a mere opinion. Mere opinions, when they differ widely from the opinions held by those around us, we often do wisely to keep to ourselves. But convictions are of another stuff. When we have them (and we don't have very many of them as a rule) we must out with them, both in word and deed, or we perish. Concealed convictions set up in the soul a moral and intellectual rot.

Well, now, you ask me, or seem to ask me, what are my views as to the amount of censorship that should be exercised over the reading of young women. That, I gather, was your particular point. More generally you seem to inquire what fruit of the tree of knowledge should still be forbidden to those of your sex after that cardinal day when they have put their hair up and let their skirts down.

Now, for once in a way, I yield to the temptation to reply by the stale rhetorical device of asking another question. What has been my practice with you, child—a practice deliberately adopted and resolutely persevered in, spite of the remonstrances of some who had every right to remonstrate, and of others who had none? Ever since you were sixteen or thereabouts—I don't remember at what age exactly it was that you began to show unmistakable proofs of marked and hereditary (don't smile!) intelligence— have you not had a free run of my library? A library, by the way, in which there is only one locked book-case, and that case kept locked, not because of the dangerous character of the contents, but on account of the expensive nature of the bindings. What happened when—but I won't go on with these tiresome interrogatives. I will just recall to your memory what happened now and then when I saw in your hands a book about which, to express indefinitely my indefinite state of mind, I had my doubts. I just looked up from my table and said, "If I were you, I wouldn't read that: it is rather dull and rather nasty"; or, "The only points about that book that have any merit are points you wouldn't understand," and, like the sensible girl you always were, you invariably put the books back in their shelves again. But I was not always in the library when you came there in search of literary refreshment, and once, only once, I remember I came upon you deep in a book about which I had no doubts at all. I noticed that you were rather more than half-way through it, and that you looked interested, though a little puzzled too. "Do you like that book?" I asked. "No—yes—perhaps—I don't know—a little," you stammered, and you blushed. Now, a blush does not in the least imply consciousness of guilt, or even of offence, as is commonly supposed. People blush not when they find themselves in the prisoner's dock, but, rather, when they are in a tight corner; more often still when they believe themselves to be suspected of something of which they are entirely innocent. When you have to deal with a child, Alexa, and you accuse it of, or question it concerning, some little delinquency, don't, should it stammer and blush, leap to the conclusion that it is guilty. But this is by the way. "Don't you wish me to read this book; shall I put it back?" you asked. "Oh, you had better finish it," I said, and turned away to my work. I did not explain to you then, but I tell you now, because it has a definite bearing on the subject in hand, that I knew that, having already got half-way through it, your interest was awakened and your curiosity excited, and I knew that in a young woman or in a young man either, for the matter of that, excited or only half-gratified curiosity is—well, I can't use too strong a term, so I will say, the very devil—the most devilish of all the legion of devils that beset the path of youth. I felt sure, too, that if I forbade you the reading of the second half of that book you would attach undue importance to what you had learned from the first half. You would see the thing—the evil thing, let us frankly call it—exaggerated out of all true proportion. You would conceive it to be worse than it really was, you would believe that it played a greater part in life than as a fact it does. Moreover, I did not feel sure—for you were, thank God, a very human girl, that you would not come back to that book when I was not there, and finish it in private, and thus do your own soul a thousand times more harm by the deception than any undesirable knowledge you might acquire could possibly do you.

You tell me that your question to me arose out of a discussion which took place a few nights ago between your host, your fellow-guests, and yourself: that it began an hour after dinner and lasted well away beyond the usual bed-time. Let me congratulate you, Alexa, on staying with such sensible people as the Mauleverers, and on being one of several guests as intelligent as yourself. By "sensible people" I mean people who are able, and who like, to talk after dinner for more than five consecutive minutes on any subject under the sun. Such people in our, or in any other class, are rare, and are, I fancy, growing rarer. It can't have escaped your intelligent observation, that ninety-nine-hundredths of the talk of to-day is about persons, and, as a rule, about uninteresting persons. The very fact that a subject is important, that it concerns us, that it has some bearing on our lives and thoughts, is sufficient to bar it out of what we ridiculously call "conversation." Is anybody interested in anything? I often ask myself on my way home from a dinner or an evening out somewhere.

But to return to this matter of the parental or guardianly censorship of books. I am convinced that if the censor could be all-wise, and managed to use his restrictive powers effectively, his censorship would work for good. But in point of practical fact, not a parent or a guardian of us all is all-wise, or is able to make use of even such wisdom as he has. An "effective blockade," as they call it in war time, over a young girl's mind is almost impossible to establish. All sorts of contraband craft will manage to escape the vigilance of the blockading squadron, do we what we may. Still, on the whole, the thing is pretty thoroughly done in France. There the novel, the novel of ordinary life, the novel written by the best and most popular writers of the day, or of past days, is never suffered to fall into a young woman's hands at all. Books for girls are things apart.

They are written by inferior authors, and as a rule are dull and insipid beyond words. The French ideal of a young woman is that until she is married her mind, so far as a certain sort of knowledge is concerned, should be a sheet of white paper. And in most French families, outside Paris at any rate, the ideal is fairly well realised. Now then, if there be any value in that ideal—if it be an ideal worth maintaining or worth following, the outcome of it ought to be that the average French married woman should have a higher standard and habit of chastity and virtue than her sister in England, where no such rigorous supervision prevails. Well, she has not, Alexa, I can confidently assure you of that. Heaven forfend that I should say a word to her discredit. She is often delightful, though not quite so often as she herself imagines. But in the matter of conduct—woman-conduct let us call it, for want of a better term—she is not a bit better than our women over here. Observe I do not say that she is worse: to say that would be to be guilty of vulgar and insular British Philistinism; but to be quite safe I content myself by saying that she is not a bit better, and consequently, is not worth all the blockading trouble that is taken with her. I have met young French ladies who have been married less than a year, and, well—I need not amplify, but my intimacy with them has left me with the conviction that it was sheer waste of time and energy to be at such pains to preserve for twenty years an innocence that four or five months were enough so completely to dissipate and to destroy.

The question, it seems to me, leads directly to the larger issue: Is knowledge often hurtful? I say "often," not "ever," for in this life there are always exceptions. For the exceptions we cannot, try we never so carefully, provide. We must, willy-nilly, be guided by general rules. In what other department of life, then, is it even pretended that knowledge, the fullest knowledge, works for ill? Can you think of one? If a traveller were about to set out on a journey through some country where grew in rich luxuriance any number of tempting fruits, beautiful to look upon, delectable to the palate, but charged with deadly poison, and certain seriously to injure or to slay outright whosoever should pluck and eat, would it, or would it not, be desirable that that traveller should be furnished with all the knowledge available as to the number and the nature of these fruits, their habits of growth, the particular places where they were most likely to be found, the antidotes to their several poisons? Would you, if you could, prevent his reading printed treatises descriptive of them, or even poems and dramas that told of them in a poetic or a dramatic way? Who would be most likely to come through the journey unscathed—the traveller who was ignorant, or the traveller who was knowledgable? Surely the questions answer themselves. It is true, of course, that even the best-instructed voyager, hard put to it by hunger or thirst, and face to face with the temptation of some specially seductive fruit, might even so pluck, eat, and perish. The clamour of his senses might prove too urgent for the resistance of his intelligence. But even so, by telling him all there was to tell, you would have done your best for him, wouldn't you? And what poor chance would the similarly-tempted ignoramus have? Well, now, every young woman is just such a traveller, and life is for her just such a journey.

On my honour, I think I have put the case as fairly and as squarely as I know how. If knowledge be our safeguard, our only safeguard, in every other of life's journeys, why in the name of all that is rational should ignorance be our best protection in this? Why should there be one little corner in the house of life in which the light shall not be suffered to shine?

You know Mr Findlater. He was here a night or two ago, and was very angry because one of his junior clerks, lately a Board School boy, had been detected in a small forgery. It was a very trifling affair, and did no harm to anyone but the poor silly lad who had been guilty of it. But Mr Findlater was full to the brim of indignation. Not with the lad—I'll do him justice in that; he didn't even intend to prosecute, he told me—but with the whole system of national education. "This is what comes of Board Schools," he declared. "You rate us for teaching these gutter brats to write, and the first use they make of their knowledge is to forge our names to cheques!" He did really, he said just that, and he is a man of not much less than ordinary intelligence! And, of course, if you come to think of it, if no one were taught to write no one could commit forgery, could they? And Mr Findlater's argument was quite as good as the arguments of those who contend that a young woman's virtue is best established on a foundation of ignorance.

And now it occurs to me that I have been wasting all the time taken in writing this letter. I feel sure that you put all this yourself, and put it quite as well, to your friends the other night. But then, you see, you have the inestimable advantage of a wise as well as a loving

Father

THE RIGHT SORT OF MAN

April 28, 19—.

My surprise is not nearly so great, my dear girlie, as you seemed to anticipate. I told you, you remember, that I was good at guessing, and I had already guessed this, or something very like this. All the same it is a blow, for a blow is none the less a blow because one sees it coming. Indeed, recollections of my sparring days seem to tell me that the blow you see coming, and from which you can escape neither by guard nor duck, is just about the nastiest of all.

Fate is a desperately skilled antagonist. It hammers us and hammers us, and knocks us out at last; but we do manage to get a punch or two back at someone or something now and then ... and that is good to remember. It is curious, isn't it, that this letter of yours, the subject of which I suppose is Love, should have set me to write about fighting? And yet ... I don't know ... they are never very far apart, Love and Strife, are they? Love is the great disintegrator, the breaker-up. See how he is coming between you and me now!

You are "not exactly engaged, but ..." I will not quote the end of your sentence, for I know how irritating it is to have one's words given back to one. Well, it is good of you to refer the final word on the matter to me. Even the most unconventional woman does wisely at great crises to respect the established conventions. Her life is made easier, less stormy so. But there! It was unjust of me to say that. I will—no, will has nothing to do with it—I do believe that in leaving this, to you so intensely personal, matter still open, so that I may have my say on it, you have not been motived by a desire to do the right, the correct thing in such cases, but by a real belief and trust in me. You have done it not because it is always done, but because you are you, and I am I, and we are to each other what we are.

But because you and I and this Third, this Third to me so shadowy, yet so portentous, to you, so substantial, are going to do all the usual things, there is no reason why I should write them to you, is there? So I will not express my gratification and my hopes, and end with a stuffy little lecture inculcating a prudential course of conduct. I will practise up the heavy-father style so as to have it all perfect by the time he (no, I will not give him a capital "h," though I note that you do) comes to see me. How I hope that at the first glimpse of him I shall feel that I may drop it. Does he expect a heavy father, I wonder. Well, if he does, he shall have one; be sure of that.

The first glimpse of him! And I haven't had it yet! It is that which has given me this queer indescribable sensation of unreality from which I have been suffering ever since I opened your letter this morning. By the way I posted your other letter to your mother on to her at once; she is staying at Richmond until Friday. One always has that curious, empty feeling when one part of one's mind fails to realise what another part of one's mind tells one is a fact. It is thus we feel for the first few moments in the presence of death. We know that it has happened, but we can't adjust our minds to the knowledge. So to-day with me. I know, or almost know, that your life, the life of all others ... but there, I will not be sentimental, so you fill in the rest ... but your life is to be dominated—well, if not dominated exactly, at anyrate directed for good or ill or half of each, by a man of whom I have never so much as caught sight, of whose very name I am ignorant.

Do you know that you forgot to mention his name? Not that it matters so long as it isn't anything very distressing. I am not afraid of that, for you know the names to which I object, and which I would rather die than have my name connected with, and I remember that you share my prejudices. We both agreed, didn't we, that Walter Pater was justified when he refused to vote a Fellowship at Oxford to a man named Juggins or something. So I take it for granted that your future name will be beyond the reach of æsthetic criticism. It ought to be a single syllable name, of course, so as to go rightly with Alexa. Christian names of two or three syllables should always be followed by a surname of one.

But I take it you have seen to that. You could not, I am sure, contemplate a life in which you would suffer from a spasm of artistic horror every time you signed your name.

Whatever he is you know well enough that I shall not be glad of him, don't you? You know that I shall wish every time I see or think about him that he had never been born. You won't mind that, because if it were not so you would feel that your father was not one of the right sort of men. Truly, I don't believe that the right sort of men ever look forward to their daughter's marriages with anything but fierce distaste. When it comes to the point, I mean. They wouldn't like them not to be married, and they hate it when they are. From which you will gather what a mistake it is to be the right sort of man, and what supreme folly it is to beget daughters, anyway.

It is rum though, rum and inexplicable, that feeling of savage resentment one has against every other man who aspires to any sort of intimacy with any woman for whom one cares even a little. Of course, one says to oneself that it is because one feels that no other man is half good enough for her. It is quite astonishing how one can lie to oneself. I know, for instance, when I can get myself for a second or two into a reasonable mood, that there must be at least a hundred thousand or so of men in England, not to mention the rest of the world, who are quite half good enough for you, and yet I hate with an incandescent hatred the mere idea, the tenuous probability that you will some day be married. If he, the unnamed and unnamable, were to come into this room now I should, or at least should try to, break him up with my bare hands and send the fragments of him home in a cab.

It was Nero or Caligula, wasn't it, who expressed the genial wish that humanity had only one head that he might cut it off? Well, I believe that at the bottom of every right-minded man's heart there is a lurking wish that all femininity were compact and personified in one woman and that she might belong to him. "Turkish?" you smile. Oh, much more than Turkish; primitive rather.

I shall not kill him, Alexa. I shall probably be tremendously nice to him if he wears the right necktie. You might give him a hint about that. One never does do the things one most passionately desires to do—they are always so outrageous those passionately desired things.

Haven't you often, when sitting at dinner, say, with a lot of depressingly correct people, ached and ached to rip out some hideous, impossible, unspeakable expression, just to watch their shocked, flabbergasted faces; and then to disappear for ever from the cognisance of man? I am sure you have; we all have. But you have never done it, thank heaven, and you know you never will. It is almost irresistible that impulse, isn't it?

And yet we resist it every time. That is because we are sane. If we yielded we should be mad; that's all. That is what sanity means, the power to resist the almost irresistible impulse. Well, I am sane, so far. I shall offer him my hand and a chair. Perhaps a cigar. I hope he smokes.

Oh yes, that reminds me. I must say just this. If he does not smoke and if he refuse wine at dinner in favour of water, or even of whisky and soda—a hateful decadent modern habit—then I will have none of him, Alexa, nor shall you. If the worst come to the worst, I will convince him by ocular and tactile demonstration that there is lunacy in our family, and I am quite certain that a fellow who neither smokes nor drinks wine will never have the hardihood or enterprise to face that. It is not that smoking or wine drinking (at dinner) are in themselves virtues, but they are indications of the only temperament and attitude towards life which are compatible with true virtue.

Mind, I will say nothing so widely embracing as that a non-smoker and non-wine drinker is not good for anybody—never mind what I think, but I will not say it. What I will say is that he would not be good enough for you; for one of us. His very presence at dinner and after would be a perpetual reproach, a constant criticism. And you would not like to be faced every evening by a criticism and a reproach.

A man who, in a world of good things, tobacco and wine and other things, abstains, is a man who makes exacting demands upon himself, and a man who makes exacting demands upon himself will inevitably make exacting demands upon his womankind.

And now, while I am about it, I may as well mention one or two other things, one or two other essentials which any man must possess before he can even begin to think of connecting his name with ours. By the way, it is you who will change your name, isn't it? What an intolerable thought that is. He must be what the Scots call "gleg in the uptak';" he must divine what you mean almost before you have said it, certainly before you have said it all. He must not, when you happen to speak a trifle elusively, stare at you blankly for half a minute or so, and then say, "I am afraid I don't quite follow you," or look it without saying it, perhaps the worst outrage of all, for the remark does at least imply a consciousness of inferiority and a sort of commendable humility.

A truly civilised woman, one of us, would rather live with a Zulu (assegais and all) who understood what she was after, than with a thing in up-and-down collars (and golf sticks) who was for ever asking her to explain herself. Heavens, how I know the look on the face of a woman after she has been married a year or two to that. No, the man who marries you must talk our language, think our thought, or there will be rocks ahead on which you and I and he will get ourselves badly grazed, not to say broken.

Then he must read and admire Henry James. I say must read, not must have read, for if he have not it may be only his misfortune and the fault not of him, but of his upbringing. The novels of Henry James (we have agreed, you remember) are the touchstone of the modern spirit. If a man can't understand them, or gets bored by them, or wishes they were shorter or less involved, then that man, whatever else he may be, is not of us or even of our time. I would rather see my daughter mated to a megatherium than to a man who could not "make out," as they put it, the novels of Henry James.

While I was on the subject of tobacco and wine I ought to have added that he must not be "anti" anything to any extent. Not anti-vaccination or anti-vivisection, or anti-clerical, or any of those things about which the faddist rages. I don't mean that he may not have strong opinions, but he must not carry them to the point of being "anti." When a man reaches that point it always seems to me he ceases to be human. A husband should be human.

And then—I had nearly forgotten this, that accursed feeling of unreality is so strong upon me to-day—he must be a man whom other women like and who likes all other women, or nearly all, all that count. I know, of course, that his voice changes and takes on another tone when he speaks to you. That is all right. But does it change and take on another tone when he speaks to the other girl? That's the thing that matters. When he hands a—oh, well, a cup, let us say, to a woman, does he do it in an altogether different way to that in which he would hand a cigar-case to a man? If he doesn't his wife will soon find herself wishing that he had never handed anything at all to her. A man's love for "the one woman," is after all only in a quintessential, concentrated form the emotion he has for all other women, the generalised thing particularised.

I don't agree with the incorrect saying that reformed rakes make

the best of husbands, but I do say that the man who has not in
him the potentiality of rakehood should never be trusted with a
wife.

But there! What does it all amount to? I write, but all the time I
am writing I am conscious that for all practical purposes I might
as well go and shoot peas at the sun as direct these wise
observations at a girl in the first bloom of what they call love. Of
course, I know well enough that just now you see in this
intrusive Third all these qualities and attributes upon which I
have been insisting. Or if you don't you think they don't matter;
and that I don't matter; and that even you don't matter; that
nothing matters but this new magic that bandages your eyes and
carries honey to your lips. Could I have chosen for you I would
have scaled the heights of heaven if haply I might bring down to
you a god, and ... you would not have liked him dear. You
would have asked for a man instead. And you would have been
right, for you are not a goddess, but a girl and the heart of my
heart: —

> *"And you must twine of common flowers*
> *The wreath that happy women wear,*
> *And bear in desolate darkened hours*
> *The common griefs that all men bear."*

Write to me again soon. Come home soon, very soon. It is a long
time that you have been away; twice as long since yesterday.

Your
Father

MODERN MARRIAGE

May 3, 19—.

My dear Alexa,—

I resist gallantly the temptation to begin much less formally, much more sentimentally than that; but I feel that marriage is the one subject on which a man may not be sentimental. In matters of marriage it is always sentiment that undoes us.

He called here yesterday afternoon, as by this time you are no doubt aware, for I feel pretty sure that as soon as he left he scribbled a note to you from the nearest post-office. If I know anything about men I know that. I should not be at all surprised if he telegraphed; but I hope not, for it is bad to begin matrimonial enterprises by a present to the Post Office.

So you see I have had a whole evening in which to think him over; a night to sleep upon my thoughts and a morning in which to recast them, as it were. When I tell you that I really did sleep and that I found my breakfast this morning not more hateful than usual, you will realise that all is pretty much as you would wish.

Yes, the man will do. Except that he is a man, and that he wants to marry my daughter, my critical eye can find no serious fault in him. Of course I wish he were dead or in some distant colony—but no, no, I don't dislike him quite so much as that last would imply—but that wish of mine means little or nothing that need worry you. One so often does wish dead people in whom one can find no fault—indeed, they are more often than not the very people one can do so well without.

I tried him by all the tests. I offered him one of my very best cigars, the sort I never have enough of in the house, and he smoked it like a fellow of taste. Even when we were talking seriously about serious matters—you are a serious matter to him and to me—he held it now and then so that the perfumed smoke could titillate his nostrils. Had it been a bad cigar and he had done that, I should have known him for a charlatan and sent him about his business.

He came in a frock coat too, a frock coat fullish in the skirts—I hope you didn't put him up to that. Had he worn one of those cut-away things that fasten with one button in the middle of the waistcoat! Words fail me as to what would have happened had he worn one of those.

He knows how to sit in an arm chair without getting into trouble with his elbows or showing too much sock. Has it ever occurred to you, Alexa, that in the matter of the disclosure of ankles a man should be as discreet as a woman?

We did not talk of you all the time. I should have learnt little by permitting that, for the veriest oaf can say the right things about a girl with whom he is in love; but we talked of books, of pictures, of music, of cathedrals, of the things that really matter, and he was all right there.

He has a good deal to learn, but then he has some time in which to learn it; and if you do justice to your upbringing he will not lack a competent tutor. There—that's the prettiest compliment I have paid you for many a long day.

Your mother was charmed with him. I rather think she is writing to you at this moment to tell you so. I confess that fact does not vastly impress me, because mothers look always with a friendly eye upon their daughters' suitors, supposing, of course, that they are anywhere near the mark.

Has it ever struck you as queer and rather significant that while women are always anxious for their daughters to marry, men, for the most part, boggle at the thought of it? It looks almost as though your sex got more out of the arrangement than ours, doesn't it? That if they stand to lose more, as they indubitably do, they stand to win more too?

The inveterate belief of women in the glory and beauty of marriage always stupefies me. I suppose there is not one married woman alive who does not know at least half a dozen others who have come hopelessly to grief in their marriages, and yet they go on believing! Such robust faith is touching and a tremendous compliment to us.

Indeed, it is a wonderful institution this marriage—marriage as it exists among civilised people, I mean: civilised Western people, I should add.

I suppose if a committee of ingenious men and women of the world had met together to devise the scheme of sex relationship best calculated to ensure unhappiness to the two parties concerned, they could not have hit upon anything more likely to secure this object ... well, perhaps not unhappiness exactly, but uncomfortableness, let us say ... than modern marriage, monogamic marriage.

From that point of view it is almost perfection. The object of it would seem to be to destroy as quickly as possible all the feelings with which people start off on it. The end, it would seem, is the negation of the beginning. Rum!

Think, now. What is it that gives the quintessential charm to that state of mind we call being in love? What is the magic of it? You can't be expected to know just now, because you are not in an analytical mood; emotion of any kind is fatal to accurate analysis.

Well then, I'll tell you. It is romance—a sense of strangeness, of something to be discovered, of infinite, thrilling, and perilous possibilities.

Why do sisters and brothers not fall in love with each other? Not because to do so would be "unnatural," not a bit of it, never believe that. Nature has nothing whatever to do with it. It is because they have been brought up together in close and daily intimacy; because there is no romance, no glamour of the undiscovered, no possibilities just beyond the horizon line.

Now marriage, as we know it, is the inevitable slayer of romance. Before the intimacy of marriage romance disappears like a mist wreath in the blazing sun.

Mind, I do not say that in losing romance you lose everything; there are many other things that are worth having, perhaps even more worth having, but you lose romance, and lose it in something less than six weeks.

And when you have lost romance you are no longer "in love." You may still love and be loved. You do and are, if all things go well with you, both; but you are no longer "in love." The very feelings which attracted you to start with, which brought you together, are gone, and gone for ever.

That is the stupendous fact of marriage; it kills the thing that made it. It is the outcome of illusion. People in love imagine that marriage is a continuance of the feelings, intensified, which they have for each other before they enter upon it. That, Alexa, is exactly what it is not. It is the very opposite of that.

Most people will tell you—one hears it said all about, especially just now—that the reason why marriage is not the success it might be is that married people "see too much of each other." There is something in that, no doubt, but there is more not in it, so to speak. It is not, I am convinced, so much because married folk see each other every day that romance takes wings; it is rather because they can make sure of seeing each other every day. It is the sense of security that kills.

I verily believe that an odalisque in an Oriental harem, for whom a visit from her lord is some sort of an event, a thing which may or may not happen on any particular day, has a better emotional time of it than the wife in a suburban villa who knows that her husband will appear at the front door, little black bag and all, ten minutes after she has heard his train puff into the station, or the still more unfortunate lady who can always get speech of him by just calling up the stairs.

Your poet Dante Gabriel Rossetti once told a friend of his, and of mine, that all those exquisite sonnets of his, dedicated to his wife and to wedded love, were written when Mrs Rossetti was away on long visits. That I can well believe, and I believe moreover that they were written not only when she was away, but when he was not at all sure when she would come back.

Once in a little walled town in the South of France I saw a play in which the husband and wife used to make assignations to meet and dine in a private room at a restaurant, although they had an excellent cook at home. It was a silly little play, but the dramatist knew something of human nature and of marriage, all the same. Poor dears, they were trying after something which they could not get, of course, but still, the very fact that they did try proves something, doesn't it?

Intimacy, security—these are the fatal diseases of marriage. I think I see you gibe a little at the word "security," and murmur something cynical about divorce. You are right in a way and wrong in another way. One has only to look around one to learn that marriage is by no means synonymous with security; but all of us, when we marry, believe it is, and so the result is the same.

Mention of divorce suggests to me to say this. I don't believe that the sort of thing which leads to the divorce court, and, where quite uncivilised people are concerned, to the Old Bailey, is half so often, as most suppose, the outcome of wilful incontinence or of sheer naughtiness, no, nor even of the waning of love. It is the passion for something that marriage does not satisfy—the passion for Romance. The unfortunates yearn, yearn with an irresistible yearning, for something to happen, something unusual, something with a spice of danger in it, something which pulls at the heart's strings, something to make one wake up in the morning with a feeling that the eggs and bacon for breakfast are not the most exciting prospect of the day. Ah, heaven! Don't we all know it—the coldest, the oldest, the most austere of us!

I formed this opinion entirely out of my own head years ago, and it was curiously confirmed by an experience of three days I once spent in the divorce court. It was when I had that tiresome Chancery suit—you remember, about Ida's marriage settlement—and I had to waste a lot of time in the law courts.

I could not sit and listen to the Chancery counsel prosing over technicalities, and so I passed the days in a court which touches human nature a trifle more shrewdly and less expensively.

In those three days I saw about a dozen cases tried and disposed of. And what sort of people do you think they were who came there with and against their wills? The gay, the frivolous, the debonnair? Oh, dear me, no; not in the least. I saw not one gallant gentleman, not one lovely lady. On the contrary, they were the dusty, the dowdy, the humdrum, and, this is the odd thing, the middle-aged! They were the kind of women who make their own hats, make them very badly, and talk about their servants at afternoon tea; and of men who go up to town at 8-45 of a morning, and come home by the 6-15. Some of them, of course, had occasionally lost the 6-15, and that was where the trouble began.

It is grossly unfair to the aristocracy to say that it is they who keep the divorce court going. "Aristocratic divorce cases," as the Radical papers absurdly call them, make not one per cent. of the whole. It is the dull, stodgy middle-class among whom immorality is rampant! And it is just because they are dull, stodgy, and middle-class.

The pleasures, the emotional outlets of art, the distractions which intelligence can always find in the world, are closed against them. Meanwhile, beneath their commonplace domesticity the passion for Romance, though smothered, smoulders on. One fine day, on the most ridiculously inadequate provocation, it bursts into a flame and then—"decree nisi with costs."

Poor devils, poor, poor devils, they haven't brains enough to outwit a Slaters' detective or even a prying housemaid.

Brains, ah! yes. Brains are your stand-by in marriage as in most other of life's perplexities, Alexa. It is brains that keep you out of matrimonial troubles, and even, when in a slack moment, you do get into difficulties, it is brains that will pull you out of them.

Looking at those of my personal acquaintances who have come bad croppers over their marriages, I find that in every case there has been want of wit on one side or the other, often on both. Brains! That is why I have considerable confidence in your future, my daughter.

One word more. Romance, in-loveness, cannot survive six weeks of the appalling intimacy of marriage. That is past praying for. What shall follow its departure then? Mere emptiness, a tramp across a sandy desert or a treacherous bog? That depends. The thing that should follow is friendship, friendship of a peculiar, a unique, sort; friendship touched by tenderness, mixed with memories, coloured by emotion.

But again remember this—it takes as much brains to build up and to maintain a friendship of that kind as it does to ... well ... more than it does to do anything else in the world so well worth doing. Fools may make satisfactory lovers, only the wise can be lasting friends.

You return on Friday, isn't it? I shall be at Paddington to meet you. See to it that He is not there—just for this once!

Your
Father

THE SUBTLE SOMETHING

June 5, 19—.

It is all right, child. I have not a word of blame, not a word of criticism even. You are valiant and original. I am sorry, of course, sorry for you, sorry for him, for myself, for everyone remotely concerned. But I am congratulatory too. I congratulate you, him, and myself. You are prepared for blame of course, for blame from everybody but your own consciousness and your own father. A young woman who engages herself to a man, remains engaged for nearly a month and then "breaks it off" when there is no conventionally agreed-upon cause for the rupture is, in the eyes of the world, a jilt. It can't be helped. It's no use grumbling. The world will have its labels—and small blame to it, they spare it the trouble of thinking, of exercising the faculty of discrimination. And we upon whom its labels are stuck, must just grin and wear them. Let us see to it that we do grin and wear them—with a grace.

That "subtle something" of which you can't say more even to me—there is no need of greater definiteness, I, as always, understand—is the true, almost the only, irremovable hindrance to happiness in marriage, the marriage of sensible people. Anything does to make fools unhappy. It is unpardonable and unforgettable. Unpardonable, because it is not a deed or even a thought or a look; unforgettable because it is always there. And the worst of it is, it can by its very nature discover itself only in intimacy. One has to jump into the water before one finds out with certainty that one can't swim. That subtle something, so colossal, so inexpugnable yet so elusive! What is it? Where is it? Is it in the blood, or in the brain, or is it some attribute of that unthinkable but must-be-thought-of entity, the Transcendental Ego? I hate to seem so grossly materialist, but I think it is in the blood, and will be discovered some day by chemical analysis, or by an improved microscopy; caught and put into a little bottle.

At present only something finer than chemical analysis, personal perceptiveness to wit, can discern it, and it must be the personal perceptiveness of the one most interested. All the others must needs be the veriest bunglers. That is why I am not kicking myself to any extent for having thought, in my blindness, my inevitable blindness, that he was all right, that he would do. He would have done for me, but how could I know that he would not have done for you? And yet I did just once have the vaguest, dimmest, shadowiest ghost of a suspicion that all was not quite well. It scurried past me that thought, that thought that was not quite a thought, across the darkness of my mind as a small mouse scurries across a dark room. It was one night when you had been seeing him off downstairs and we were all in the drawing-room. When you came back I caught a look upon your face ... no, something less than that ... just a flicker across your lips ... and it made me uneasy, gave me a tiny twinge in that rickety old heart of mine, it kept me awake for an hour or two, as a mouse, fidgeting, has often done.

I am glad of one thing though; that except in the matter of which I could not judge, I did not judge him wrongly. He is made of the right stuff. I had a letter from him last night—a letter from a man to a man. He doesn't whine, he doesn't rage, he doesn't wrangle. He doesn't even complain. He accepts the inevitable. I think the final test of a man is his attitude in face of the inevitable. I will never show you that letter—of course you would not wish it. I feel in a curious way as though it were I and not you who had hurt him.

Once more then, my daughter, you are right. You have done well. Let no misgivings on that point ever gnaw or even nibble. There are not many things that can justify the breach of a betrothal deliberately entered upon. That subtle something is one of them. Had the case been reversed, had it been he instead of you who had made the discovery, I should have said the same.

Now let the subject be dropped for ever. We will not even refer to it, no, not by a look, when you come home next week.

Your approving
Father

THE END